Getting Through to Your Kids

Getting Through to Your Kids

Talking to children about sex ▪ drugs and alcohol ▪ safety ▪ violence ▪ death ▪ smoking ▪ self-esteem ▪ and other critical issues of today

Michael H. Popkin, Ph.D.,
and Robyn Freedman Spizman

A Perigee Book

A Perigee Book
Published by The Berkley Publishing Group
A division of Penguin Putnam Inc.
375 Hudson Street
New York, New York 10014

First Perigee edition: March 2002

Published simultaneously in Canada.

Visit our website at www.penguinputnam.com

Library of Congress Cataloging-in-Publication Data

Popkin, Michael, 1950–
Getting through to your kids / Michael H. Popkin and Robyn Freedman Spizman.
p. cm.
Includes bibliographical references and index.
ISBN 0-399-52750-8
1. Parent and child. 2. Communication in the family. 3. Moral education. 4. Values
clarification. 5. Decision making in children. I. Spizman, Robyn Freedman. II. Title.

HQ755.85 .P67 2002
649'.7—dc21   2001052392

PRINTED IN THE UNITED STATES OF AMERICA

10 9 8 7 6 5 4 3

NOTE: Every effort has been made to ensure that the information contained in this book is complete and accurate. However, neither the publisher nor the author is engaged in rendering professional advice or services to the individual reader. The ideas, procedures, and suggestions contained in this book are not intended as a substitute for consulting with a professional. Neither the author nor the publisher shall be liable or responsible for any loss or damage allegedly arising from any information or suggestion in this book.

While the author has made every effort to provide accurate telephone numbers and Internet addresses at the time of publication, neither the publisher nor the author assumes any responsibility for errors or for changes that occur after publication.

To our children who manage to raise our spirits,
while we are busy raising them.

Contents

Acknowledgments

We are deeply indebted to our editor, Sheila Curry Oakes, for her wonderful guidance and insightful reading of our manuscript and to our literary agent, Meredith Bernstein, for her outstanding efforts and unyielding assistance helping to make this book a reality.

From Michael: Thank you to my wife, Melody, and children, Megan and Ben, for your encouragement and support of my efforts to write this book. Thank you also for your insight into many of the topics addressed. I also want to express my appreciation to the staff of Active Parenting Publishers for their loyalty and support while I worked on this project. A special thanks to Marianne Adair, catalog manager at APP, for her help in selecting the books for the resource section, and Rachel Metzger, director of Product Development.

From Robyn: To my loving husband, Willy, and children, Justin and Ali, who have allowed me to be an expert at getting through. To my dedicated parents, Phyllis and Jack Freedman, Gus Spizman, Sam Spizman, Doug and Genie Freedman, Lois and Jerry Blonder, Ramona Freedman, my wonderful family and friends, who continue to make all of my efforts so worthwhile and meaningful. Thank you for indulging twenty years of my literary endeavors and a special thanks to my mentors and dear friends Drs. Stephen and Marianne Daniels for their professional support and friendship. I wish to also thank the wonderful staff at the Spizman Agency including Tara Marvos, Hilary Munson, and Amy Klein for their valuable support, and to Bettye Storne, to whom I remain eternally grateful.

Chapter 1

Bringing Your Message Home

Seven-year-old Tori is playing with her LEGOs while her parents try to catch a few minutes of the evening news as they hurriedly get dinner together. The lead story, a biological attack by terrorists, catches young Tori's curiosity for a moment, then recedes back into the shadow land of adulthood. Later, at the dinner table, something that one of the TV anchors said rises back into Tori's conscious mind. A concerned look etches onto her innocent face, and, between bites of chicken fingers, she nonchalantly asks, "What is anthrax?"

Twelve-year-old David lies silently in his bed. His red-streaked eyes stare into the darkness of his bedroom. It is the same bedroom that he has slept in almost every night for the past five years. Only now it seems strangely different, a lonely mausoleum where angry shadows dance against cold, hard walls and taunt him. The next morning, during a silent breakfast, he looks up from his uneaten bowl of cereal and angrily asks his mother, "Why did you make Dad leave?"

Fifteen-year-old Carrie, after months of playing the role of unlik-

1

able misfit at her new school, has finally found a group of friends to hang out with. Okay, so they're not the smartest kids in the school, but they know how to have fun, and frankly, Carrie figures she deserves to have some fun after so long without it. On a cloudy afternoon in one of their basements while his parents are out, one of Carrie's new friends pops open a can of beer, takes a long drink, then passes it to the girl next to him. She takes a swig, then passes it to the next. Before long it is in Carrie's anxious hands. Nothing is said, but somehow Carrie knows that her chances of staying a part of this new group are a lot better if she just goes along. Plus, it looks like fun. So, head back and eyes closed, she takes her first swallow. That night at the dinner table she thinks about her experience. She does not ask her parents a thing.

Never before in modern history have children been exposed to so much so young. Terrorism, drug use, sex, and a host of other adult concerns now share center stage of our children's imagination with Captain Hook and Harry Potter. Television, movies, the Internet, and other forms of modern media have opened windows to a world that for most of our history was reserved for adults. Since we can no longer shield our children from this information, we had better be ready to help them make sense of it in a way that builds values and not just knowledge.

The steady bombardment of messages that we receive each day has led our era to be dubbed the Information Age. The sheer volume and clutter of these messages make it difficult for any single message to get through clearly and with impact. For parents trying to fight through the competing values and beliefs represented in this barrage in order to stake a beachhead in their children's minds, the task can be overwhelming. Yet we persevere knowing that the battle for our children's minds is the challenge we accept when we become parents. If we are lucky, our children will ask us questions that give us opportunities to help them make positive value-oriented interpretations of this complex world. Yet, these questions are often the stuff that can make a parent's face turn red and her knuckles white.

What do you say to a seven-year-old who asks about oral sex? How can you help a twelve-year-old who is struggling through the divorce of his parents? And perhaps most important of all, how do you get through to your child about all those matters that they think about, but never ask you about, like the teenager wondering about her first beer? All too often we subscribe to the outdated notion that "no news is good news." We mistakenly believe that if our children are doing okay in school and not getting into trouble, then all is well. We feel confident that our rules and our discipline are sufficient deterrents to the misbehavior and harm that we know is lurking. Yet are our kids safe?

A recent statistic indicated that drug use was down among teenagers. However, at the same time, it was on the rise among eighteen- to twenty-four-year-olds. What does this mean for parents? It is possible that it might mean only that parents are finally getting through to today's teenagers, and that yesterday's teens, who were more reckless, are today's young adults. However, there is another, more alarming conclusion to be drawn. It is also possible that parents have improved their ability to control their teenager's behavior while teens are home under parental rules and regulations, but as soon as their kids leave home, these same kids throw caution to the wind and become reckless. Without parents there to ground them, in more ways than one, many young adults do not seem to have the inclination or ability to avoid many of life's temptations.

When parents are only concerned about behavior, their kids do not form the necessary attitudes, beliefs, and values to make sound judgments when left alone. The old autocratic parenting methods that relied on reward and punishment and a "because I'm the parent and I said so" mentality do not give children the foundation to deal with a world of increasing complexity and variant values. If you want your children to make decisions based on moral thinking and take into account the potential consequences of their actions, it is necessary that you invest the time in talking with them about everything from current events and how to handle problems with friends to why smoking, drinking, and drugging are things to avoid. How to do this in a way that truly gets through to your kids is a matter of two things: your overall relationship with your child and your ability to communicate effectively. Whether or not you want to communicate with your children, you can't avoid it.

You Cannot NOT Communicate

An ancient Zen student wrote to the master, "I have written you sixty-eight times and you have not answered. This, too, is an answer." The truth about communication is that even our silence sends a message. Add to this the subtle nuances of voice tone, facial expressions, gestures, and other nonverbal cues, and we are always sending out messages. No wonder our children pick up our beliefs and values even when we try to avoid telling them anything. Unfortunately, when we are unintentional in our communication, what they pick up is not always what we want to communicate. This reminds us of the old joke, "I know you think you understand what you thought I meant to say, but I'm not sure that what you think is what I thought I had said."

This book is about the intentional communication of values and beliefs from parent to child. To be sure, you will still communicate much unintentionally, but by having short, pointed conversations with your children on a regular basis, you will increase your ability to influence the beliefs and values they are forming.

Taking the time to talk with your kids about important topics is the first step in becoming an intentional parent. Your wisdom and experience can be a lighthouse on the rocky coast for children trying to steer a safe course on a stormy sea. On the other hand, you can also cause a shipwreck. Children, especially teenagers, strive for independence. If your child feels bullied or pushed into a corner, or feels that you are cramming your own outdated values down his throat, the result will often be rebellion. A dictatorial or overbearing approach may very well push your child into an oppositional position whereby he does the exact opposite of what you want in order to avoid being pushed around. This urge to rebel against autocratic parenting can be so powerful that we sometimes feel the need to advise teenagers to "have the courage to do what you really want to do, even when it's also what your parents want you to do."

In chapter 2 you will find ideas for successful communication, ideas that will improve the likelihood that your talks will lead to cooperation. You have much knowledge, experience, and wisdom to share with your children, and they want to hear it. But they also want to know that the ultimate decision for their lives is in their hands. This book will help you balance this delicate partnership and enable you to get your messages through to your children effectively.

What Do We Tell the Children?

Childhood is a time of questions. From the benign "Why is the sky blue?" To the poignant "Why do people die?" To the provocative "Did you have sex before you got married?" kids are wondering and often asking about how the world works and how they can best be a significant part of it. It is as if life were a game without a rulebook. Kids want to succeed at this game, so they constantly look for information about how the game is played and how it can be won. To the extent that they respect and trust us as parents, they will ask us questions hoping to better understand how it all fits together. This affords us a wonderful opportunity to help them get it right. It can also be a knee-knocking experience for even the most confident parent. You swallow hard, take a deep breath, and wonder, "What should I tell him?"

This book is divided into content areas that will help you think about what to tell your children on a variety of common issues in today's world. Drugs, sexuality, divorce, violence, illness, death, money, and a host of other topics come expertly packaged with the sage advice only available to those of us with multiple initials after our names. All you have to do is open the book and read aloud to your child, and she will magically be transformed into a bastion of good sense, moral reasoning, and mental health. Of course, if you are not rolling your own eyes right now (or at least chuckling), then maybe you should. This book contains information, ideas, and suggestions based on years of experience working with parents and children. It is grounded in modern theories of child psychology and development and, where applicable, includes the thinking of others experienced in their fields. However, since every child is different, what works with one child may not be effective with another. This means that *you* are still the ultimate expert in parenting your children. When your own still-small voice tells you that something in this book is hogwash, we suggest you listen. We are not saying that it *is* hogwash, only that you have to live with yourself and we don't. Plus, if you don't believe something is correct, you are not likely to be able to sell it to your children. So, as one impertinent mother once told me during one of my seminars, "I use the best and let go of the rest." We hope that you will be as wise.

We also hope that you will accept that our children have the same philosophy about us. They realize parents have a lot to offer, but they learn soon enough that we are not perfect. In fact, nature did not put them here to be our clones or Mini-Me's. The human species grows and evolves through change. Our kids look similar to us, but different. They may have similar aptitudes and talents, but they will have different aptitudes and talents, too. They may adopt some of our values, but they will challenge some of them as well. Ultimately, they will become their own selves with abilities, looks, and a philosophy of life of their own. We can help influence this process, but we cannot control it. By providing useful information and opening a dialogue with your children, we can help them choose wisely, but it is a mistake to think that we always know what is best for them.

A Few General Guidelines

Before even considering the specific information that you might want to share with your children about various topics, let's go over some general guidelines that apply to all areas. What do you tell the children when you really want to get through?

1. TELL THEM THE TRUTH (AS YOU SEE IT).

Credibility is a key to influence. Only when we trust that what someone tells us is true are we willing to open ourselves to being influenced by his or her leadership. If you don't trust what a political leader tells you, you are going to resist, on some level, being influenced by what she says. If you don't trust what your boss tells you,

you are unlikely to follow his leadership with much vigor, if at all. If your kids lie to you about their behavior, you know how hard it is to trust what they say for a long time into the future. *And* if you lie to your kids, even with their interest at heart, you erode their confidence in you as a source of reliable information in the future. They may still ask you questions and listen to your answers, but the stock that they put in those answers is weakened, and your ability to help shape their attitudes and values is reduced.

It is sometimes difficult to be honest with our children and still protect their feelings. What do you tell the child who asks fearfully, "Are you and Daddy going to get a divorce?" Even if your marriage is on solid ground and you have a high degree of confidence that it will stay that way, telling your child what she wants to hear—"No, honey, we're not going to get divorced"—may wind up not being the truth at some later point. No one can control the future, so let's not lie to our kids and pretend that we can. An honest answer might be something like "I know it's scary with so many parents getting divorced these days, but Daddy and I love each other very much, and we work hard at having a good marriage. We both plan to stay married, and I don't think anything is going to change that."

2. TELL THEM THE TRUTH, BUT NOT NECESSARILY THE WHOLE TRUTH.

Parenting does not take place in a court of law with one hand on the Bible. Telling your child the truth does not mean that you have to share every nook and cranny of your life experience or answer every question asked with total candor and completeness. It will depend on the age of your child, his level of maturity, and your own personal values. For example, what if your teenager asks you if you ever had sex on the first date? While the whole truth might be "Yes I did. In fact, more than I really should have," you probably don't want to be this candid. In fact, you may not want to answer the question at all. Here's one way to avoid dishonesty without giving your child information that will probably not be helpful *and* at the same time still open up a dialogue:

"I don't believe that parents ought to share the details of their sex lives with their kids, but I'm glad to see that you are thinking about sexual behavior. What do *you* think about having sex on the first date?" (All the while thinking, "Please God, don't tell me you've done it already!")

Let's take another example. In the days following the first terrorist attacks using anthrax, a father was talking with a friend in the presence of his thirteen-year-old daughter. He wanted his daughter to be well informed and was telling them both about a lecture he had recently heard, which had been given by a biological warfare expert. The essence of the message had been that since anthrax is a bacteria, it is treatable and only a limited threat. However, if terrorists ever got their hands on smallpox, a virus that kills 30 percent of those who contract it, THAT would be a big problem.

As the father continued to enlighten his daughter about the risk of a smallpox attack, she grew strangely quiet and muttered, "I don't want to hear this."

"We can't keep our heads in the sand," the father replied in an attempt to encourage his daughter.

But this was too much for her and she rose angrily saying loudly, "I'm only thirteen years old! I don't need to know everything!"

To his credit, the father knew his daughter was right and backed off. In fact, her words are an eloquent reminder that even precocious children and teens are still not adults. They lack the emotional and psychological maturity to handle some information and should not be force-fed more than they can digest. A good rule of thumb is to tread lightly, taking your cues from your child as you proceed. Asking if the child is all right and "Do you want me to keep going?" can help give the child permission to end the talk. It is also usually less threatening to start with the big picture and only give the details that your child can handle, offering reasonable reassurance as you go.

3. TELL THEM WHAT THEY HAVEN'T ASKED ABOUT.

If you are fortunate enough to have a child who trusts you enough to show you the high honor of asking you a question, then by all means make the most of the situation. Your child's question is an attempt to tap into your vast resources of knowledge and experience. This doesn't mean giving them a twenty-minute lecture, but rather bridging from their initial question to the unasked questions that often lie behind the original query. The late psychologist Chaim Ginot used to say, "Children speak in code." In other words, their questions are coded messages about what is really on their minds. For example, we are all aware of the hidden intent behind such a question as "How much does the new PlayStation cost?" when what they are really asking is "Can I have one, can I can I can I . . . Pleeeeeeeeze?" But the child who asks, "How many people smoke in America?" may really be saying, "I'm thinking about smoking. Do you think it's a good idea?" If you only answer the surface question, then you are missing an opportunity to help your child think through an important decision and form helpful values. Using the original question to bridge into a full discussion of smoking is a golden opportunity that should not be missed.

4. TELL THEM YOU CARE.

There is an old expression among counselors that "people don't care how much you know until they know how much you care." While this may not be true when it comes to such emotionless subjects as repairing the computer or asking for directions, it is absolutely accurate when it comes to human interaction. We tend to trust people's advice and perspective a lot more if we feel that they have our best interests at heart. This is even truer for our children.

When kids think that we are telling them about drugs, sexuality, or any other concern to make *our* lives easier or to maintain the status quo, they tend to not only want to reject our advice, but to sometimes do the opposite of what we want them to do. It is only when we communicate that we are coming from that place in our hearts that truly loves and cares for their health, safety, and happiness that we have a chance to influence their thinking and help them learn to discipline their natural desire for fun and excitement. How you communicate this caring is not just a matter of words. Sure, it's good to say, "I love you. I care about you. I want to see you grow up healthy and happy." But even more important than the words themselves is the attitude that lies beneath the words. Kids are quick to discern insincerity. A bogus attempt at concern is going to backfire amidst rolled eyes and incredulous sighs.

If years of family hassles and unresolved conflicts have made it hard for you to remember how concerned you are about your children and how much you really do love them, think back to the first time that you held your child as an infant. Think about how you discovered in a single moment just how deep a love you could feel for another human being. Remember the sheer joy that you felt at this tiny life that was now nestled safely in your arms, dependent on you for his very life. You had it once, and you can recapture it again. If you need help with discipline and guidance, as most parents do, there are books and courses that can help you build the parenting skills to reduce the stress between you and your children. This will also, as one parent put it, "help reawaken the joy I felt for my child." Whatever you need to do to get there, remember that you are most influential when you come from your love for your child and not your authority as the parent. Authority may be great for managing behavior, but when it comes to getting through to their minds and values, you need the psychological connection that true caring can help build.

5. TELL THEM WHY.

Did your own parents ever look you in the eye with that steely stare that parents can do and say those infamous words "Because I'm the parent and I said so!"? And did it warm the cockles of your fuzzy little childhood heart? Or did it plant a seed of discontent and rebellion? For most kids today, the power play of blind authority has become a challenge to rise up and throw off the yoke of parental tyranny. While their rebellion may be covert (ever wonder how some kids can drag out getting to a bath for twenty minutes?), it almost always leads to frustrated parents and children. Worse, attempts to lead without reasonable answers robs us of the credibility we will need to influence their attitudes and values. Only when our children see us as intelligent, thoughtful human beings who have learned through life experience information that can help them make their own lives better are they willing to open their minds to our influence.

Our parental authority is not the issue here. We certainly do have the authority to make decisions where health, safety, and family values are concerned. This is our responsibility, and we need not apologize for doing our job. At times most parents need to back up that authority with appropriate discipline. But the *authority* to govern behavior is not the same thing as the *ability* to influence opinion. Winning over our children's and teens' minds requires sound reasons and persuasive arguments. This was one of the problems with the "Just Say No" antidrug campaign of the 1980s. Just telling kids to say no without giving them meaningful reasons why to say no is only going to be effective with kids who already believe that drugs are bad. The rest just laughed at the campaign.

There are times when just giving your child the necessary information is enough to help her make sense of a difficult situation in a way that helps her mature. For example, when a five-year-old asks why Mommy isn't home tonight, it may be enough to tell her in a calm and loving way, "Remember when we you told you that Mommy was going to the hospital to have an operation and she would be away for a few days? Well, tonight's the first night. I thought we might make her a 'get well' card. Would you like to do that?"

There are other times, however, when you will want to help influence the attitude that your child is forming. In matters such as tobacco, alcohol, drugs, sexuality, and violence, for example, you will want to arm yourself with some good information and strong arguments. This book will help you think persuasively about these and other areas. However, there are many other resources available to you for reinforcing your goals for your children. Begin collecting articles, books, and videos and look for movies and TV shows that help make your case. When possible, enroll your kids in schools and other programs that reinforce your values. The more good reasons that come from many people your child respects, the more likely your positive messages will get through.

6. TELL THEM CLEARLY.

There is a saying that "clarity leads to power." Think about the speeches that you have heard in your life that truly got through. From John F. Kennedy's inaugural address and Martin Luther King's "I have a dream," to the pep talk given by a high school football coach or the words of wisdom from a trusted teacher, confidant or parent, chances are that those that were remembered had a clarity of focus that gave them uncanny power.

On the other hand we have all experienced the boredom and fatigue that sets in when someone is muddling through a presentation with no clear understanding of what he wants to communicate. Without a clear focus, the speaker's own energy and passion becomes diluted leaving both him and his listener grasping just to stay tuned in, much less to remember what was being said. When we do not have a clear message to send to our children, we wind up saying things like "I'm not sure that is such a good idea," or "I'm not sure I'm really comfortable with that." This lack of clarity is accompanied by a lack of power that offers the child little direction or guidance. A much clearer and more powerful answer might begin "I don't think that's such a good idea because . . ."

When you do not have enough information to give a clear and powerful response, ask clarifying questions of your child until you become clear. You may sometimes need to say, "I'm still not clear about this. What can we do to get more information?" The key is to stick with it until you get enough information to give a clear response to their questions, whether asked or unasked. This may mean using the resource chapter at the back of this book to help you learn more about a subject. It may mean thinking about your own values and what you truly want for yourself and your children. Once you make these decisions, think about how you can clearly communicate your message to your child. Some people find that making some notes beforehand helps them assemble their thoughts clearly. Others prefer to just concentrate on the message mentally until they have a clear idea about what they will say. Whatever works best for you, remember that clarity leads to power, which in turn leads to getting through.

7. TELL THEM THE FACTS *AND* THE VALUES.

It is almost amusing that the most famous of all parent-child talks is code-named "the facts of life." Although the facts related to reproduction are certainly important for kids to know, the beliefs and attitudes that underlie their thoughts and actions are even more important. Perhaps this often dreaded conversation about human sexuality should better be labeled "the values of life." Unfortunately, most parents gloss over the values and focus almost exclusively on "the birds and the bees," another misnomer. While it is very important to get the facts right, it does a child little good to have this information if he has a poor understanding of how to use it respectfully within a value system that serves him, others, and the community as a whole. Our children are busy developing the attitudes and values that will shape a philosophy of life from which they will make countless decisions during their lifetimes. What do you want your son to do when he is at college and a group of guys invite him to join in having group sex with a consenting young woman? What would you hope that your daughter would do when some of her girlfriends try to entice her to sleep with a cute guy just for kicks? Talking with kids about value-oriented choices can help them develop the emotional muscle to stand up to pressure—whether inside themselves or from peers—later.

The Goals for This Book

In each chapter of this book we will help you think about your own values and how you can talk about them intelligently with your children. At times we will provide questions to open discussions with your kids. We will also present some of the facts that you will want to share as part of these discussions. After all, facts and values are often interwoven to make good choices. For example, it is a fact that AIDS is transmitted through sexual activity. It is also a fact that this is a deadly disease with no known cure. These two facts have become a vital part of how many people have changed their values regarding sexuality. A lot of people who once valued unprotected recreational sexual intercourse now shun such activity as unsafe or even stupid.

Sometimes there is not enough information to call something a fact, and we have to go with our opinion on the matter. For example, some people have the opinion that recreational sex cheapens the satisfaction that two people who love and are committed to each other can achieve through sexual intimacy. This opinion, like all opinions, may or may not be a true fact. However, as a parent, you will want to share your opinions as persuasively as possible with your children in an attempt to counter some of the opinions they will be hearing from peers and other sources. Even so, it is worth remembering that nature did not allow us to clone ourselves for a good reason. Our children's values will not be an exact replica of our own.

This book will also include many of the difficult questions children ask their parents today. It will include many more that remain unasked but thought about. Although the answers to these questions will be a product of your own values and beliefs, we have offered some examples in each case to prompt your thinking and get you started. This list is far from exhaustive, but it does not shy away from the tough ones. If you have a specific problem area in your family, such as a learning disability or chronic illness, you will want to consult the resource chapter for more in-depth materials on the subject. Finally, there are problems in which outside professional help is required. Your words will always be important, however, there are times when the resources of doctors, psychologists, educators, clergy, and other experts can be invaluable. We encourage you to use such helping professionals when problems do not improve or interfere to a large extent with everyday living. There are times when it takes a team to get through. And the value of teamwork is seldom overrated.

Chapter 2

How to Get Through

Grandpa Joe is in the hospital suffering from complications resulting from congestive heart failure, diabetes, and alcoholism. The doctors have him in intensive care, but his chances for recovery are not very good. His daughter, Karen, and her husband, Chris, have two children, Sarah, fourteen, and Greg, ten. Karen has taken a leave at work so that she can spend much of every day at the hospital keeping her dad company and hoping to talk to the doctors whenever they make their rounds. Chris has been very supportive himself, coming to the hospital often and doing double duty at home. The kids have never had to deal with a life-and-death problem before, and Karen and Chris wonder what to tell them. Should they tell them how serious the condition is or shelter them as long as possible? Should they ask the kids to visit their grandfather or spare them the possible anguish of seeing him on a ventilator with tubes, wires, and bags of strange liquids attached? Should they mention the alcoholism at all?

Keisha, ten is playing on a soccer team for the first time.

Although a good athlete, soccer skills are not easy to master, and she is discouraged at not playing better or being a starter in the games. One day at school a friend asks Keisha to come to the friend's birthday party on Saturday. The plans are exciting and Keisha really wants to go. Unfortunately, the party conflicts with Keisha's soccer game and she can't do both. Keisha tells her mother that she is going to the party and that she wants to quit soccer anyway. Keisha's mother wonders what to tell her daughter. Should she let her quit? Should she make her miss the party? Should she compromise and let Keisha miss one game, but not quit the team?

These are two different situations with a number of important things in common. Both require the parents to make important choices about what to tell their children. Both offer wonderful opportunities for teaching values and influencing attitudes as well as behavior. Both require some skill on the part of the parent about *how* to tell the children in a way that really gets through.

Don't Just Tell Them . . . Sell Them

These two situations are also very different. The first involves a delicate life-and-death issue complicated by one of the great challenges facing parents: how to steer their children away from alcohol. However, it is simplified by the fact that the parent's job is oriented toward giving their children helpful information. The second situation, although less important, contains the added dimension of putting the parents in a spot where they may want to exercise their parental authority and limit their child's behavior while at the same time persuading the child that it is the right thing to do, and furthermore, that doing the right thing is in her long-term best interest. This *persuasive* aspect of parenting is the difference between *selling* our values and *telling* them. Most parents can limit behavior with a few good lessons in discipline, but selling a point of view is more challenging and potentially more rewarding.

Values are not usually formed in a single moment, but are built over time as the child gathers more and more evidence to support a point of view. Situations such as these two examples offer what are sometimes called teachable moments when parents have a golden opportunity to strengthen the formation of positive values and attitudes. In fact, even in the first situation, the parents have the opportunity to teach (or persuade) their children about a number of issues including the use of alcohol, taking good care of one's health, and even the meaning of life and death.

The Beauty of Dialogue

When the ancient rabbis assembled in Persia to write the Talmud, the Jewish book of religious law and ethics based on the Old Testament, they talked for days, months, years, and decades before concluding what they thought was right. (This, by the way, without playing a single hand of bridge or ordering out for pizza.) Today when a modern family sits down to have a discussion about something beyond the scope of what movie to go see, they are lucky to keep everyone's attention for ten minutes. Our hurried little moment in history has robbed us of many things, and one of them is all too often the intellectual dialogue that serves to sharpen values and refine opinions. The give-and-take of ideas exchanged between family members serves as a test ground for children to try out new ideas in a safe environment. It strengthens their intellect by helping them develop the ability to formulate ideas and opinions built on facts and common sense. It builds their courage and confidence by confirming that their ideas are valued and that their opinions matter. It reminds them that they are grounded in a family, a family that thinks. And perhaps most important of all, it becomes the crucible in which the child's value system and philosophy of life can adapt and form within the influence of loving family members.

Three Steps to Helping Kids Get It

Whether the dialogue is between just you and your child or whether it includes others in the family, or even friends and relatives, there are three steps that will help you talk to children in a way that gets through.

STEP 1. Ask and listen.

STEP 2. Give your opinions persuasively.

STEP 3. Talk about consequences.

These three steps can make the difference between a one-sided "blah blah blah" conversation in which the kids roll their eyes and tune out and a dynamic talk that helps you instill useful information and values. As you read these steps you will find that you already know many of these ideas. We encourage you to build on this current base by adding the tips and methods that fit your own developing style. Let's look at each step more closely to see what they really mean.

STEP 1. ASK AND LISTEN

Sounds simple enough, but it is surprising how often we get so caught up in what we want to say that we forget to hear what our kids have to say. This is especially easy to do when our kids give us that familiar "I dunno" when we do ask them a question. The following three keys will help you start a dialogue and keep it going while at the same time helping you open your child's mind to your influence:

A. Ask good questions.

B. Listen actively.

C. Listen with empathy.

Mastering these three keys will make you a better communicator with your children and with anyone else. Let's see how they are done:

A. Ask good questions

The biggest mistake that most parents make when it's time to talk with their children about important matters is to turn the conversation into a monologue, or worse yet, a lecture. The problem with monologues and lectures is that unless you are a late-night talk-show host or acclaimed university professor, you probably don't have much experience with either monologues or lectures. Consequently, you aren't very good at them, and you'd probably bore your child, as well as yourself, to death trying.

On the other hand, you probably already know how to ask good questions. If not, it's a lot easier to learn than captivating an audience with a gifted lecture. Plus, questions have the added value of provoking dialogue, and we've already lectured you on the value of that. If you need more convincing, consider the wise words of the Roman smart guy, Zeno of Citium, who said, "The reason we have two ears and one mouth is that we may listen the more and talk the less." Listening to our children talk is a very encouraging thing for us to do. Plus it provides us with information about how their values are forming and where we might want to support or redirect them. It lets us know about their feelings and how these feeling might play out in behavior. And good questions are the keys to getting kids to talk.

What's a good question? To begin with, good questions cannot be answered with a simple yes or no. They require elaboration, and therefore open up dialogue.

While asking yes or no questions might be fine for trial lawyers intent on trapping hostile witnesses, it is disastrous for parents trying to instigate a conversation with a child or teenager. Instead, try asking the *how, what, when,* and *why* questions that are *open-ended* in their ability to promote discussion. For example, instead of asking the closed-ended question, "Do you think using drugs is dumb?" and getting a simple "yes," a better question might be "What are some reasons why using drugs is dumb?" This gets your child thinking and opens up a dialogue. You might even add a creative role reversal and ask an even better question: "Let's say you were a parent who wanted to get across the idea that using drugs is dumb. What are some reasons you could give your kid?"

TIPS FOR ASKING GOOD QUESTIONS

The following tips can help you ask good questions that promote discussion without damaging your relationship with your child:

1. **Ask open-ended questions (how, what, when, and why).**

2. **When asking "why" questions, be sure that you are asking for information and not interrogating the child.** For example, not

"*Why* do you think that?", which might be taken as a challenge and make some children defensive. A better question would be "*What* are some reasons that might be true?" Since *why* questions are often about a person's motivation, they can be seen as confrontational and invasive. It is usually better to ask them about other people and not the child. For example, "*Why* do you think that some people use drugs even though drugs are dumb?"

3. **Ask questions that focus on others, not your child. For example:**

   - After watching a movie together, "What mistakes do you think that the victim made that led up to the ending?"
   - What could she have done differently?
   - How did the drugs play a part in her destruction?

4. **Ask general questions to get a sense of what your child already knows and how others are influencing him. For example:**

   - What have they taught you in school about smoking?
   - What do your friends say about it?
   - What do you know about cancer, heart, and lung disease?

5. **Ask questions that help your child put actions and consequences together.** For example: "How do you think that his decision to steal the car affected his life?" or "What was the effect of her getting drunk at the party?" We will talk more about the importance of consequences in Step 3, but helping our children learn the relationship between our choices and the consequences that follow is helpful at any time.

B. Actively listen to your child

Once you have asked a good question, it is time to listen. But how you listen can be for better or for worse. Here, we can learn something from those professional counselors and therapists who have studied the art of listening. The concept of *active* listening is now legend in these circles. The era of passive listening in which therapists sat back in a comfy armchair, rubbed their chins (this is not a grammatical error as they often had two or more chins), said "uh huh" a lot, and were justifiably satirized in movies is long gone. Today's helping professional is a lean, mean listening machine who sits forward, focuses not only on his client's words, but on facial expressions and body language, and responds in complete sentences.

Parents who want to establish an open dialogue with their children will do the same. Giving your child your full attention is encouraging. It motivates her to want to share. After all, who wants to share her heartfelt questions and concerns with somebody who is half-listening to you and half-thinking about last night's football game or tomorrow's carpool schedule? Active listening also means listening with your eyes as well as your ears. You will be surprised how much information you can pick up through your child's facial expressions, body position, and tone of voice. In fact, the words themselves carry only a small percentage of any communication, and training ourselves to get the entire message is particularly important because of questions that have not been asked or perhaps even thought. You have to play detective looking for the clues that tell you what is really on your child's mind and what information she needs to handle and learn from the situation.

C. Listen with empathy

Did your own parents ever couch bad news (like "No, you can't go to the movies, you have to stay here and finish your homework") in those famous words "I'm only doing this because I care about you"? If so, I bet it didn't help. And yet, they were on the right track. They probably did have your interests at heart. They also knew that if you understood that, then you wouldn't hate them so much for saying "no," and that they could set limits on your behavior (a parental responsibility) without ruining the relationship. The problem was that saying the words "I'm only doing this because I care about you" does not communicate the message in a way that most children get.

Remember that most of any communication is nonverbal. For your child to really feel that you are on his side and have his interests at heart, he needs to get that you care about his feelings (including his wants, likes, and dislikes) here and now, and not just in the future when "you'll thank me later." This is critical, because if he does not get that you are on his side, then your persuasive arguments and the information that you want to deliver in Step 2 will fall on either deaf ears or ears that have run to his bedroom crying.

If you want your words to get through to your child when it's your turn to speak, it is almost essential that you learn to *empathize* with your child in the present moment. This means understanding what your child is feeling, caring about those feelings, and if at all possible, feeling them yourself. To do this, put yourself in your child's shoes and ask yourself, for example:

- How would I feel if I couldn't go to the party because I had to stay home and do homework?

- How would I feel if my grandfather were critically ill in the hospital?

- How would I feel if my parents were getting divorced?

This doesn't mean that your child will feel the exact same thing, but if you check out their body language, facial expressions, tone of voice, and words, you should get a pretty good idea. Once you sense what your child is feeling, let him know that you have an idea "what it's like to be me" by responding with a word that describes his feeling:

"I can tell you are really *disappointed* that you have to stay home."
Or
"I can hear how angry you are about missing the party."

If you are not sure what your child is feeling, make your empathy statement tentative. That way if you are off, your child can correct you with no damage done to the communication. For example:

"You *seem* very *sad* about Grandpa."
"I *guess* you are pretty *angry* at me for divorcing your father."

It is important that your own facial expression, tone of voice, and body language are congruent with your words. This means, for example, that saying, "You seem very sad about Grandpa" with a tone of voice and facial expression that says, "But I don't really care how you feel" is not going to help. You have to really feel for your child and let your face (especially your eyes) and your voice communicate those tender feelings. Again, putting yourself in your child's shoes can help you get the right perspective.

One of the positive results of empathy is that it encourages the child to continue sharing. When people feel understood and cared for, they want to open up. What they are opening up is more than just their mouths. It is also their minds. This enables us to influence their thinking and sets the stage for Step 2.

STEP 2. GIVE YOUR OPINIONS PERSUASIVELY

There are a number of well-intentioned parenting authors out there these days teaching parents how to be successful dictators of behavior. These writers have a few very effective methods for getting kids to knuckle under to parental authority and do what they are told when they are told to do it. As we said earlier, this is not that difficult an assignment. What is difficult is getting kids to believe that what we want them to do is in their best interest so that they will choose to do it on their own someday. This is the building of ideas, beliefs, attitudes, and values that lead to what is commonly called *character*. Another definition of character might be this:

Character is the integrity to do the right thing even when you could get away with doing the wrong thing.

Since we are not always there to ensure that our children will do the right thing, it is important that they develop the character to do so on their own. As such, character is different from fear. Doing the right thing out of fear of getting caught and having to pay the consequences is only valuable to a certain point. For individuals and society to really prosper, people must be willing to do right because it is right in the larger sense of being good for others as well as us.

Dictators, whether they run governments or families, rarely sow the seeds of character. What they reap is more often lying, sneaking, and black-market trading if not out-and-out rebellion. Research by social psychologists has shown that when children are given large rewards or threats to behave in certain ways, they do not accept inner responsibility for the consequences. Instead, they attribute their compliance with this outside stress. Consequently, when the outside stress is removed, they go back to doing the negative behavior. On the other hand, when minimal outside stress is used, the children seem to internalize the message and believe it even after the stress is removed. Samuel Butler put it this way more than three hundred years ago: "He who agrees against his will/ Is of the same opinion still."

We are not suggesting that you ignore misbehavior nor relinquish your responsibility to discipline your children according to the needs of the situation. What we *are* suggesting is that you go beyond discipline toward developing the ability to persuade and teach your children how to think about the slings and arrows of life's outrageous fortunes in ways that build healthy minds and solid character. This means that you have to *sell* your values to your children, not just *tell* your values. Getting through to our children so that they *get* it means presenting ideas in ways that enable their minds to accept rather than reject those ideas. Asking good questions and empathizing with their answers helps you open their minds to your point of view. The following tips can help you build on this foundation to become more influential teachers.

TIPS FOR BEING MORE PERSUASIVE

1. **Build your credibility.** The more your child respects you, the more she is likely to respect your opinion. Many parents have become better people knowing that this is true and wanting their children to look up to them. The more you model your values through positive behavior, the more your children will see you as a credible source of guidance. The more your opinions come from knowledge and sound information instead of blind authority, the more credibility they will place on your opinions.

   Being credible does not mean that you have to become a

perfect person. In fact, there are times when you can even use your own mistakes to help persuade your child not to do the same. For example, "I know I haven't always made good choices in my life, and I know I don't have any right to tell you what to do in this area. But if there is anything that my mistakes have taught me, it's this. . . . My hope for you is that you can learn something from my mistakes that will save you from some of the pain that I have caused myself and others." Such an admission of fallibility, when accompanied with a genuine feeling of remorse, can actually increase a person's credibility in an area.

2. **Develop good reasons that are relevant, not random.** Find good information that can help you build a persuasive argument. Rather than say, "Drugs are bad," give them some good reasons why drugs are bad. People usually need personal reasons before adopting a particular point of view. This is what is known as *relevancy*, and it is so important that it has become a sort of buzzword today along with its opposite, *random*. When kids say that something is random, they are saying that it has no meaning for them and is not worthy of their attention. When something is *relevant*, however, it means that there is some use in the information that makes it worth hearing. Look for reasons that benefit your child and tie into her values. For example, if she is into sports, then talk about the health and fitness aspects of staying drug-free. Does he want to get into a good college? Then be sure to include the argument that a drug conviction would go on his record and eliminate many colleges that might otherwise accept him.

3. **Use outside resources to help build your case.** Doing your homework does not mean that you have to become an expert

on the topic. There are plenty of books, videos, articles, movies, and television programs that can be useful in presenting both the information that you want to get across as well as the values that you support. We have suggested some in the resource section at the end of this book, but you can find many others yourself. One especially powerful method is to take a class together with your teen. You can learn together about topics such as drinking, drugs, driving, money, or many other topics that you want to cover. The group support of such experiences is another powerful factor in helping you influence your child's values.

4. **Use stories and metaphors to create an "aha" experience.** There are two sides to the brain, right and left. The left is more susceptible to rational arguments, facts, and figures. The right is more intuitive and is more influenced by stories and images. Although some people tend to be more left-brain– or right-brain–oriented, it is usually a good idea to work toward getting through to both sides. However, young children are especially right-brain dominant. They love narrative and are captivated by a good story that they will request hearing or seeing over and over again. To young children, a story is almost like having the experience itself. And since experience is the most powerful way to get through at any age, a good story can help you get messages of value through to your children very effectively. Even with older children and teens, the ability to project oneself into the action vicariously opens the mind to the "aha" experience of truly getting a message for the first time.

Take time to find and read books to your children that help teach the beliefs and values that you want to reinforce.

31

Bible stories, *Aesop's Fables*, and a host of modern books are available on every topic in this book and countless more. As your kids get older, take turns reading out loud with them, finding books that are appropriate for their age and reading level. While reading together has the added benefit of strengthening their reading skills, you can also find excellent stories available on audio and video that can create the added emotional appeal that opens the mind to influence. Be sure to build on this effect by talking with your kids after the story is over, emphasizing the key messages that you want to encourage.

Akin to the storytelling aspect of getting through to the right brain is the use of metaphor. A metaphor is a visual image that can graphically and emotionally represent a more abstract concept. This helps lock the message into the right brain at an unconscious level as well. For example, a football coach once called his team into the locker room for a meeting. He then put a bag of cocaine on his desk for the team to observe. Next, he emptied a white pillowcase in front of the team. Out crawled a poisonous rattlesnake. The team jumped back in fear. "I understand why you jumped away from that rattlesnake," said the coach. "But what I want you to realize is that cocaine is just as deadly, and when you see it, you need to think of that rattlesnake and get as far away as you can."

The coach had created a graphic metaphor of a rattlesnake for the abstract words *cocaine is deadly*. Do you think the message got through? It is doubtful that any of the players who were in the room that day would ever even hear the word *cocaine* without seeing that rattlesnake again. While we don't recommend using deadly snakes to create metaphors with children and teens, literature is filled with vicarious metaphors that will get through and stick. For example, we all know that "crying wolf" is a metaphor for pretending to need help just to get attention. And we know the consequences of crying wolf was getting eaten by the wolf. The story of the little boy who cried wolf might be the most remembered literary metaphor ever created, but you will find thousands of others if you look. And of course, you can always create your own.

5. **Use emotional windows to enter your child's mind.** Significant emotional events have the power to open a person's mind to change faster than anything else. A sudden traumatic event can influence entire belief systems to the extent that there is a complete change in personality. On a smaller scale, an emotional experience creates a window in which new beliefs and attitudes can be formed much more readily than at other times. It is not up to us as parents to create those significant emotional events; however, when we see one happening, we want to take advantage of the opportunity to teach. These so-called *teachable moments*—from skinned knees to hurt feelings—are precious opportunities to use the communication skills previously discussed both to support your child empathically and to provide information that will get through profoundly.

6. **Use endorsements.** We have all learned to look to the opinions of those that we admire to help us sort through the confusion of information that we are bombarded with every day and to help us determine the right thing to do in ambiguous situations. Sometimes this is as unimportant as checking the movie reviews before choosing which picture to go see. Other times it is very important, such as making career choices or even deciding whom to marry. Be especially on the lookout for people your child admires, whether sports heroes, entertainers, or people in your community. Their opinions will carry great

weight and can help persuade your teen to go against peer pressure or internal desire when the going gets tough.

7. **Encourage positive beliefs.** Look for any words that seem to be moving in the direction that you want your child to go and reinforce the underlying belief by making an encouraging statement such as: "That makes sense." "You make a good point." "Good thinking." "Yes." "I didn't think of that, but it's an excellent idea."

8. **Get your child to commit, preferably in writing.** Commitment is a powerful tool in determining our behavior and strengthening our beliefs. For example, let's say that you believe that a certain candidate is slightly more desirable than another. If you are asked by someone who you support and why, and you express your support for this candidate, afterward you will be even more likely to believe he is the best and vote for him. If you express your positive feelings to a group, you will become even more committed. And if you write an article and have it published, then you will increase your commitment even further. Why? Because there is a very powerful human tendency to be consistent in our opinions, especially when we have made a public commitment. Work at getting your child to make small statements of agreement and work up to larger ones. For example, when discussing driving, you might ask, "Would you agree that driving a car is dangerous and should be done so very carefully?" Most teens would agree with this, especially if you have shared any of the statistics on teenage accidents. Once they have agreed, they become more committed to safe driving. To increase this level of commitment even further, negotiate a contract with your teen and then sign it together. (See chapter 4 for an example of this.)

9. **Get your child to do the research and to persuade you.** Instead of you always trying to persuade your child to accept certain beliefs and attitudes, a very powerful persuasive technique is to get her to persuade you. This builds on the desire to be consistent, so that once she has argued for a certain position, she will be more likely to adopt other beliefs that support this position. For example, in the area of drugs and alcohol, you might say the following to a young teen:

"Like all parents, I worry about the dangers out there that can hurt you. For example, I know of so many kids who have ruined their lives or even died because of using alcohol or other drugs. For me to feel good about you going to parties and other places where kids might bring these things, I need to feel certain that you understand just how dangerous drugs are and that you are committed to staying away from them. So, here's what I want you to do. I will pay you an extra week's allowance to go online (or to the library) and research why teenagers should avoid alcohol and drugs and to present your arguments to your dad and me like we were teenagers. If you can convince us not to use alcohol and other drugs, then we'll be okay with you going to parties and other places."

Make sure your teen makes the report in writing and verbally. Ask questions challenging her a little so that she has to argue convincingly against alcohol and other drugs. Afterward, tell her what a good job she has done and that you'd like to send a copy of her wonderful work to friends and relatives. Make sure she is okay with this, but if you can get her to agree to make it more public, you will increase her commitment to the arguments she has made. We have included a list of Internet sites that you can give your child for each topic. And if you cannot get her to do the research alone, then you can do it together. (A word of warning: Do not offer to pay too much for the research or threaten with severe consequences if she doesn't do it. Remember, the less outside stress necessary to get her to commit, the more she will internalize the experience and agree with the opinions later.)

10. **Utilize the power of repetition.** Advertisers know that they have to put their message in front of a person as many as ten to fifteen times before the message gets through. With so many competing messages vying for attention, there is little way that a single message will get through. The exception is if that message is accompanied by a significant emotional experience, which is why teachable moments are so important. However, we cannot always wait for emotional experiences to teach the values and attitudes that our children will need to form character. Memory is also formed by repetition. The more our children hear a message, especially from many people using various channels (for example, books, videos, talking, music, and classroom discussion), the more that message is ingrained in the child's memory. Look for opportunities to repeat messages in as many ways and circumstances as you can find. When your child finally gets sick of you repeating yourself, you'll know that the message has gotten through.

STEP 3. TALK ABOUT THE CONSEQUENCES

We have said that the most powerful influencer of beliefs is direct experience. When we experience the consequences of our behavior directly, we have a lesson that is difficult to ignore. A child stubs his toe running carelessly across a concrete driveway and experiences the painful consequence of his actions. The next time he starts to run across the driveway, an alarm sounds in his mind, and he remembers the painful experience. He slows down and makes sure his toes point slightly upward. The rest of his life he never stubs his toe again. Ah, if only all of life's lessons could be learned so easily.

There are two general categories of consequences: natural and logical. Each can be tremendously helpful for influencing our kids behavior and beliefs. As behavioral scientists have long known, what happens immediately after we do something, the consequences, will help determine what we do in the future. Let's think about each type of consequence and how it can help us get through to our children.

Natural consequences

Consequences delivered by Mother Nature without the aid of parents or teachers, such as stubbed toes, are called *natural* consequences. They can be very powerful teachers, but as the saying goes, Mother Nature can also be quite a witch. Consider the four teenagers out joyriding with an unlicensed driver who loses control and crashes the car into a brick mailbox. The natural consequences of their reckless behavior included the deaths of two of the teens. The obvious problem with some natural consequences is that although they are profound teachers, the outcome is sometimes so catastrophic that the educational value is lost on the victims. (You can be sure that the two survivors learned a lesson about driving that they will never forget, and that the lesson may have extended to friends and even those who heard about the accident later.)

Because the consequences of teen misbehavior can often lead to such tragedies as car crashes, drug overdoses, pregnancy, and even murder, it is up to parents to help them learn from the consequences of other people's mistakes. There is an old saying that there is no substitute for experience. In fact, as we have said, we do learn best from our own experiences. However, there is also no substitute for someone else's experience. We humans also have the ability to learn vicariously from other people's mistakes. Any talk that you have with your child or teen about issues involving health and safety should include discussion about the possible consequences of various attitudes and behavior. Since having a few poignant real-life examples can strengthen your case, collect news articles, tape television reports, and find other ways to share the lessons learned the hard way by others.

However, many kids, especially teens, often think that this "potential" just will not happen to them. This nothing-bad-is-going-to-happen-to-me syndrome is what keeps us parents waiting up at night until our teens are safely home. Using your persuasive skills to break through this foolish denial will work for some kids. Others need a consequence that is real, rather than potentially real. This is where parental discipline through the use of *logical consequences* can help.

Logical consequences

Logical consequences are those results that a parent imposes on a child in order to limit negative behavior. The word *logical* means that the consequences are connected to the misbehavior in a way that makes sense, and not just an arbitrary punishment. For example, a teen caught driving without her seatbelt fastened might experience the logical consequence of losing the privilege of driving for a period of time. A teen caught smoking might not be allowed to go to parties or other social events for a period, since there is a higher risk of smoking at these functions. To be most effective, logical consequences should be delivered in a firm, yet calm, tone of voice and be discussed with the teen beforehand.

A discussion of consequences should also involve the benefits of positive behavior. For example, in addition to the health and safety benefits of not smoking, you might also point out that they will look and smell better, have much more money to spend on other things, and earn the respect of many other people. If you have a teen, you can add that many people only like kissing nonsmokers. As we stressed in the "persuasion tips" section, it is important to encourage their own positive comments and behavior with your own words of praise. For example, phrases like the following can help build the positive values that you want to encourage:

"I agree."
"Good idea."
"Yes, that makes a lot of sense."
"That shows a lot of maturity."

Simply nodding your head affirmatively as they talk and saying "uh-huh," "I see," or "yes" can subtly reinforce your child's positive beliefs. The more these beliefs and values are reinforced, the stronger they become. And strength of values is important because they will be tested.

Chapter 3

Building Core Values and Strengthening Character

Two young adults walk into two separate banks at exactly the same time to cash checks. In both cases, a distracted teller mistakenly gives back 25 percent too much change. The two young people are of similar means and circumstances. Each is single, making ends meet, and has no unusual circumstances such as a hungry child to feed or a sister who desperately needs an operation. Each immediately notices the mistake and is momentarily elated at the prospect of such a financial windfall. A moment later one's face contorts slightly as if feeling a sudden tug from within. "I think you gave me too much money," the lucky customer says, as he pushes the extra money back toward the surprised teller. At the same instant, the other young adult is quietly pocketing the extra cash without hesitation. As they exit their respective banks, each is smiling, feeling very satisfied with the situation.

What accounts for people of similar circumstances behaving so differently in similar situations? The short answer is their beliefs, attitudes, and values. In even shorter terms, their character. Remember, character is both the sum total of our beliefs, attitudes, and values, as well as the integrity to do the right thing even when you can get away with doing the wrong thing. Both bank customers could have gotten away with keeping money that wasn't theirs to keep, but only one of them had the character to give it back. Let's look at the three elements underlying this important concept more closely:

"Beliefs" can be defined as that which we think is true without absolute evidence. For example, both bank customers may have believed that it was wrong to keep the extra money and that they would probably get away with it if they just keep quiet.

"Attitudes" reflect a person's posture toward something. For example, both customers had a positive attitude toward money. But one customer kept the money and the other gave it back. Why? Because of their values.

"Values" refer to how worthwhile we believe that something is. What is the value that these bank customers place on money? How much do they value honesty? Do they value doing the right thing more than doing the expedient or fun thing? Because values are often in competition with other values, the stronger values usually win out in producing behavior. For one customer, this led to giving the money back, while for the other it led to keeping the money. Each left feeling satisfied, because each was operating within his own value system.

Let's look at a parenting example. Let's say that you want to influence your child not to smoke. There are probably a number of competing values and beliefs that go into the equation. Each of these values can be weighted from 1 to 10 depending on how strongly it is held. Let's see how they might compete in determining a teen's decision about smoking. For example:

VALUE 1. Having friends. (Strength of value: 9 out of 10)

BELIEFS: These kids like me and I like them. Not that many kids like me, so I don't want to blow it with this group. They smoke and will probably like me better if I smoke, too.

VALUE 2. Staying healthy. (Strength: 5)

BELIEFS: Smoking isn't good for me, but I don't think it's as bad as they say. Besides, I can always quit later.

VALUE 3. Keeping the respect of parents. (Strength: 2)

BELIEFS: My parents only talk to me when they don't like what I'm doing. They yell and put me down all the time, so who cares what they think.

VALUE 4. Freedom. (Value: 5)

BELIEF: If my parents catch me smoking, they'll ground me. But I won't get caught.

VALUE 5. Being attractive. (Value 8)

BELIEFS: Cigarettes make your teeth yellow and your breath smell bad. But it looks cool.

Given these values and beliefs, it is predictable that this teen will have a positive attitude toward smoking. What will determine if he actually begins smoking? Opportunity. In fact, we might state it as a formula:

Positive attitude + opportunity = action

Since the opportunity for high-risk behavior is so prevalent these days, it often comes down to a matter of attitude on the part of youth. This is where having a positive set of core values can be, well, *invaluable*. "Core" values are those values that are fundamental to our personalities and highly resistant to change. They are often formed during childhood through many experiences and frequent reinforcement. However, sometimes a single highly charged emotional experience such as a trauma can account for a core value in an instant. For example, a victim of a violent crime can come to value personal safety very highly and very deeply after an attack.

What are some of the positive core values that can help our children develop the character to make wise decisions later? Some examples include:

health	honesty	respect	
safety	compassion	perseverance	
courage	hard work	joy	
learning	humor	love	
reason	charity	friendship	
cooperation	responsibility	moderation	
wisdom	family	spirituality	
freedom	excellence	money	character

What values would you add or delete from this list? Which are most important to you in your value system? How will you look for ways to encourage them in your children, especially while they are young? For example, you can see how having a strong core health and safety value might make it easier to develop a negative attitude toward such risky behavior as drugs, unprotected sex, smoking, and drinking in excess. However, if the health and safety value were *too* strong, it might negatively compete with the values of joy and courage by making the person too fearful to take reasonable risks. This is where a *moderation* value can be helpful.

To encourage positive core values, look for opportunities like the following to encourage them directly in your children or vicariously through others.

Tips for Instilling Positive Values

1. **Read and discuss stories with positive values.** Stories such as *Aesop's Fables* help teach positive values through characters that are easy for children to understand. Read such stories to your children and discuss afterward. You can also find excellent audio and video stories to share with your children that also reinforce your values.

2. **Live it; don't just give it.** Children learn best by watching, and they are often watching you. What you model through your behavior, and how you encourage them to live is much more influential than words alone. For example, if you want your kids to value helping others, then plan family activities that involve volunteering in the community. If you want them to learn moderation as a value, then avoid behaving in excess.

3. **Prioritize your time and money to reflect your values.** There is an old saying that if you want to know what a person really values, do not listen to the tongue in his mouth, but watch the tongue in his shoes. In other words, our behavior tells others what we truly value. This is especially true about how we spend our time and money. If you value *family*, then make sure that you spend time with your family. Most people would not

rank *television* as one of their core values, so don't let it be a thief of time that you might spend with your family or in other more highly valued activities. Your actions will communicate volumes to your children and those around you.

4. **Talk about positive and negative values in the behavior of others.** Whether characters on TV or in real life, children can learn a lot about life and the importance of various values through family discussion. If a character in a movie was dishonest, talk about that dishonesty in a negative way. For example:

"When he started lying, he had to keep lying to cover up his lies. You could tell how bad it made him feel, but he didn't have the courage to stand up and take his consequences, so he suffered guilt for lying. Then he finally got caught anyway and paid an even bigger price because then nobody could trust him."

In this brief commentary on a movie, the parent has not only reinforced the core value of *honesty*, but also *courage* and *conscience*.

5. **Provide a loving spiritual education for your children.** A loving (as opposed to harsh and moralistic) religious experience can help build many of the core values listed above. A good teen youth group can also add a strong buffer against many of the negative values that compete with what you want for you child. When I produced the video documentary *She Said Yes: The Unlikely Martyrdom of Cassie Bernall*, the remarkable story of one of the victims of the shooting at Columbine High School on April 20, 1999, I was tremendously moved by the positive power of Cassie's youth group to help her change from a hurt and rebellious teenager into a positive role model

for millions. The response to this video was so overwhelming that we followed up with a second production, *Lessons from Littleton: Teens Reaching Out*. This story documented the impact that positive teens can have on each other as well as the community. Helping your teen find positive peer groups can pay tremendous dividends, and a religious youth group will work to strengthen positive values at the same time.

6. **Help your child be around other positive role models.** No child learns everything she needs to know from her parents. Even the most conscientious parents need help. Look for opportunities to put your child under the influence of other role models who share positive values. Notice that we didn't say who share *your* values. While you probably don't want your kids under the influence of neo-Nazis, it is also unwise to insist that every adult that they learn from has an exact replica of your value system. That is, unless you are perfect. If you aren't perfect, then there is room for diversity. Your child can benefit from having a wider range of positive values to choose from. Coaches, teachers, relatives, and friends can all be important role models to your children. Cultivate these relationships, always looking out for opportunities to associate your child with adults who can help you teach positive values through their words and actions.

Teach, Don't Preach

When we talk with our kids about important topics such as those covered in this book, we have the opportunity to influence their beliefs, attitudes, and values. However, it is important that we do not turn our kids off to our point of view by coming across as too preachy. When kids feel preached at, when we come across as know-it-alls who are trying to put them down and run their lives, they are likely to dig in their heels and resist our messages. Make sure that there is always a give-and-take to your discussions. Listen to their value statements and find ideas to agree with. It is this common ground that will give you the credibility to influence their beliefs.

Act, Don't Just React

Many parents wait until their child asks a question before tackling the tough issues addressed in this book. While such an invitation is certainly advantageous, we can no longer afford the luxury of just sitting back and waiting for our children to initiate these conversations. Such a *reactive* style of parenting is just too risky in an era where kids are facing life-and-death choices. Today's world calls for active parenting in which we anticipate problems beforehand and take proactive measures to prevent them. The information presented in this book will give you a leg up in taking such action. Make the time to have pointed conversations with your children individually or as a family on topics covered in this book and others of your choosing. Do this regularly and it will become a routine that will provide rich dividends for your relationship, as well as your peace of mind.

How to Tell When You Have Gotten Through

Answering your child's questions, initiating conversations, and using the other methods in this book to build positive beliefs, attitudes, values, and character in your children is not a perfect science. Sometimes your words will get through and sometimes they won't. The proof is ultimately in the choices that your children make going forward. Their behavior will be the ultimate feedback. However, you can also get an idea of what is sticking and what is not through additional talks. Wait a few weeks or months following a talk, and then bring the subject up again. To see what got through, ask one or more of the following questions.

"Do you remember that talk we had about _____ a little while ago? I was thinking about it again and wondering:

- "If you were a parent, what would you want to be sure that your child knew about _____?"

- "How would _____ (for example, "using drugs") make your life different?"

- "If you and I were to write a book about it, what is the most important thing that we should tell parents and kids about _____?"

The answers your child makes will give you a good idea about what got through and where you need to reinforce your message. Be careful not to become critical or judgmental. This is not a test and you aren't giving grades. It is for your own feedback, so that you will know where to go next.

Your Words Will Go with Them

The remainder of this book will help you consider what information to share with your children and ways to share it effectively. This information is not intended to be exhaustive. There is much more than can be covered in a single book, but we hope that it stimulates your own thinking about ways to help your child build the values, attitudes, and beliefs that will lead to positive behavior, happiness, and character.

There may be times when you wonder if your words have been of any help at all. Your kids may argue and seem to reject the very heart of your message. In fact, there will probably be times when you feel like you have blown it completely. Take heart. First, because parenting is too difficult to do perfectly. We all make mistakes (just ask our own teenagers!). The important thing is that we learn from our mistakes and persevere. The other fact that we find so hopeful is that our messages, even the ones that our kids seem to reject now, do find a way into their minds. Often, when these same rejected messages are heard again, from a book or a movie or another person, they make an impact that is much greater than had we never said a thing. Our kids may not even remember our words consciously. They may even believe that they have come up with the idea completely on their own. This is a way of owning one's values that is helpful, a way that should be respected. This is not the time to say, "I told you that you'd understand when you got older." It is a time to smile warmly and keep quiet, knowing that your words will always go with them.

Chapter 4

Alcohol and Other Drugs . . .
the coast-to-coast "traffic" jam

Twenty-four-year-old Kevin takes a long drag of a cigarette, then crumbles the burned-out butt into an empty beer can. Three beers and he feels a whole lot better. The stress of the day seems to fade behind his glassy eyes as he turns the key in the ignition and puts leather to metal. The car screeches against the pavement like a wounded animal, and then bolts for the road too fast. Kevin loves the sensation of speed. The excitement of hugging the road in a blur of metal and chrome kicks his adrenaline and lets him know that he's alive. Fumbling for another beer, he looks down just as the light turns yellow. When he looks back up, he sees her standing in the intersection, like a deer frozen in his headlights, unable to move. Instinctively he slams a foot into the brake. The sound of rubber screams against the concrete in a desperate cry. The car spins, a full 90 degrees, and slides toward the helpless victim. Kevin winces, agony shooting though his arms and legs as he fights for control. The car hurls sideways, unable to stop itself. The woman's eyes widen as the impact approaches. In her mind's eye she sees her daughters playing on the swings behind her house. She wonders what they will do without her. And then to her amazement, for the love of God or gravity, the car stops.

Later, a shaken Kevin sits in his apartment and marvels at his luck. Maybe he is charmed after all. Or maybe he just has catlike reflexes that enable him to do things other mortals could never hope. Still, he shakes at the closeness of the call and wonders why the beer doesn't soothe him. He wonders. It's been so long since he last did a heroin ball. Maybe it's time to take out the old horse and give her a ride. After all, he was feeling lucky and, to tell the truth, needed a little something extra today.

It was two days before anybody found his body. Two more before the funeral where everyone talked about what a great person he was and how he loved to write and how tragic his untimely death had been. But nobody got up and told the truth about the life-destroying stuff he put into his body and how he had chosen death a little piece at a time until it had collapsed in upon him like the crushed metal cockpit of a crashed car. Somebody should have stood up and told them all. There is no such thing as "a charmed life" where this stuff is concerned. Just luck. Dumb luck. The kind that usually runs out too soon.

What Parents Need to Know

You need to know two things as clearly as you know your own name: 1) We have a huge drug problem in the world today, and 2) None of our kids are immune. If you have any doubts about either of these statements, please return to your home planet. Your visa has expired.

The movie *Traffic* was considered a big eye-opener for many people in this country. The visual images of middle-class kids from affluent neighborhoods using hard drugs such as cocaine, heroin, and crack; becoming addicted; running away from home; prostituting themselves to buy drugs; spiraling downward toward an abyss many thought was reserved for the inner city and kids from "bad" homes, while the drug czar and all the government forces could not save them, amounted to a giant wake-up call for our times. Whether we will stay awake or hit the snooze button and roll back over remains to be seen. But in the meantime, there is much that we can do as parents to keep the so-called war on drugs out of our homes.

Like any war, we need to understand the enemy. These include ignorance, complacency, intolerance, and sensation-seeking. Ignorance, because what you don't know about alcohol and other drugs can kill your kids. Complacency, because to assume that although you experimented with everything under the psychedelic rainbow and emerged unscathed that your kids will be as lucky is like playing Russian roulette, winning, then handing the gun to your teenager. Intolerance, because when you crack down on your kids' individuality when it expresses itself in harmless ways, you invite them to rebel in ways that are much more potent, and potentially lethal. And sensation-seeking, because at its heart, the problem with alcohol and other drugs in our society is one of seeking more and more stimulating pleasure and excitement. We are a society that in many ways has become too tame for our genetic nature. When our kids do not have healthy ways to unleash their biochemical desire for adventure, they often turn to simple chemical ways. In fact, one of the best ways for you to help prevent the use of alcohol and other drugs is to make sure that your child or teen has plenty of healthy adventure in her life. Sports, clubs, Scouts, and other adrenaline-producing activities can give kids the excitement they seek without risking their lives.

One of the sad truths about life at the beginning of the twenty-first century is that alcohol and other drugs are easily available to kids in communities from rural to urban, impoverished to rich, and across all color lines and ethnic orientation. We are a drug-infested culture. If drugs were rats, we'd all catch the plague and die. But herein lies the good news. Drug abuse is not carried by fleas riding the backs of filthy rats waiting to jump you in the dark with the bubonic plague. Drug abuse almost always requires the conscious choice of the victim to invite the rats into his life and give the fleas ample chance to bite. Although millions do abuse alcohol and other drugs, costing our society billions of dollars and countless heartaches, the vast majority choose to avoid the rats and live clean and healthy lives. What allows some people to "just say no" to the rodents while others can't get enough of them? And what can we as parents do to help our kids belong to the first group and not the latter?

First, we need to understand that drug abuse is partly behavioral and partly genetic. As many as 90 percent of teens and preteens experiment with the use of alcohol and other drugs. Because these substances impair judgment and reduce inhibitions, these teens are immediately at risk for all kinds of catastrophes from car wrecks (20 percent of all teen driving fatalities are attributed to substance abuse) to violence (in one study half of the college students who were victims of violent crimes were using alcohol or other drugs at the time of their victimization) to teen pregnancy and HIV infections (16 percent of teens use condoms less often when drinking, and among binge drinkers, condom use is 300 percent lower, placing them at greater risk of HIV infection and pregnancy). Once a teen begins experimenting, he also becomes at risk for addiction, a downward-spiraling personal hell that destroys the lives of millions.

Fortunately, most experimenters do not become addicts. They learn to use in moderation or give it up completely. Although there are probably many factors at work in determining who becomes addicted, it is clear that some people have a genetic makeup that makes them much more susceptible to addiction to alcohol and other drugs than most of the population. Even with a deadly substance like cocaine, less than 1 percent of those who have tried it become regular users or addicts. For example, alcoholics have a genetic makeup that makes them about four times as likely as others to become addicted. If you have a history of alcoholism or other drug addiction in your family, it is important to talk to your kids about the need either to avoid alcohol (as well as illegal drugs) altogether or at least to be especially careful about limiting the amount he drinks when he becomes of legal age to drink at all.

Teen Drug Use in the United States

According to the University of Michigan's "Monitoring the Future" study, by the time today's teens have reached the twelfth grade 80 percent will have tried alcohol; 49 percent marijuana or hashish; 16 percent amphetamines; 11 percent LSD; 11 percent Ecstasy; 9 percent powder cocaine; 4 percent crack cocaine; and 2 percent heroin. That amounts to 54 percent who have used any illegal substance. If this surprises you, you are not alone. Parents almost always *underestimate* both the availability and use of alcohol and other drugs by teenagers. What's perhaps even more shocking than these statistics are the ones showing the use of drugs among eighth graders: 52 percent have tried alcohol; 20 percent marijuana or hashish; 10 percent amphetamines; 4 percent LSD; 4 percent Ecstasy; 5 percent powder cocaine; 3 percent crack cocaine; and 2 percent heroin. It is obvious that our kids are at risk at younger and younger ages. What was once the proving ground of the rebellious few is now the parade ground of the masses. Alcohol and drug use among teens is now, ironically, normal behavior. The fact is that it is still also dangerous behavior.

What Kids Need to Know

The good news is that parents can still make a difference. A recent study by the National Institutes of Health (NIH) found that by letting their kids know that they would be very upset if their kids used drugs, parents were able to significantly reduce such drug use among their children. Armed with a little information and some persuasive arguments, parents can make an even greater difference. What's more, even if your arguments do not yield 100 percent success and your child eventually experiments with alcohol or other drugs, she may remember your words later and choose to give up such use before becoming injured or addicted. The following questions can help you initiate a conversation with your child about this critical problem.

Questions to Initiate a Talk

- I've read that 80 percent of teens have tried alcohol by the time they reach the twelfth grade even though it's illegal and dangerous. What do you think about that?

- What have you heard about why it's smart for teens to avoid using drugs?

- Why is alcohol more dangerous than most kids think?

- Did you know that the marijuana available today is much stronger and more dangerous than that used twenty years ago? What problems can that cause?

- Why do you suppose that the beer commercials always show the happy, sexy people drinking and never the burned-out alcoholics and crash victims?

- Which do you think has more alcohol: a 12-ounce beer; a 5-ounce glass of wine; or a 1-ounce shot of whisky? Did you know they each have the same amount?

- Why is addiction such a terrible thing?

Questions Kids Sometimes Ask (and Possible Answers)

Q. *What's the big deal about drinking?*

A. I know it's hard to appreciate that alcohol is dangerous when you see so many people in our society drinking. And the ads they run make it look cool, fun, and harmless. Maybe if they showed one of those beer-drinking toads getting drunk and then eaten by a snake because his perception was shot and his judgment impaired, it might be different. But all we ever see is the fun side of drinking. So here are five good reasons not to drink as a teenager and, if you choose to drink as an adult, to drink in moderation:

1. **It's illegal to drink until you are twenty-one.** You don't need a criminal record, and besides, what right do you have to break the law just because you feel like it? If you break the law, it better be for a very good reason.

2. **Your brain is still developing; at least we hope it is.** Alcohol use, especially heavy use, can interfere with that growth and make you dumb. Did you know that even with college kids, those who make D's and F's drink three times as much as those who make A's?

3. **Alcohol impairs judgment and perception.** You think you are okay when drinking, but your reflexes and judgment are really off, so when you try doing dangerous things, you run the risk of catastrophe. For example, when teens drink, they are more likely to crash a car, get into a fight, commit a crime, abuse a date or be abused by a date, and all kinds of other dangerous stuff. Remember what happened to . . . (insert a personal story about somebody your teen knows).

4. **Alcoholism.** The younger you start drinking, the more at risk you are for becoming an alcoholic. (If you have a history of alcoholism in your family, add something like this: Plus, we have a history of alcoholism in our family, which means that you are about four times as likely to become an alcoholic as somebody who doesn't. This means you have to be especially careful not to build up a tolerance to alcohol by drinking to get high. Once you get high, you are building up your tolerance so that it takes more and more alcohol to reach the same high. This takes you one step closer to addiction.)

5. **This shouldn't matter as much as your health and safety, but if you need any more reasons, you should know that we will be very upset if you drink before you are twenty-one, and then only in moderation, never to get drunk.** There will also be consequences from us if you break this rule.

Q. *But everyone drinks these days—why can't I?*

A. Because you aren't a sheep, you are a person. This means you don't have to follow the sheep in front of you into the slaughterhouse. You have the ability to think for yourself. Never—and this applies to a lot of things, not just drinking or using drugs—never think that just because a lot of people are doing something that it is necessarily the right thing to do. History is filled with examples of when going along with the crowd turned out to be either foolish or an outright disaster. Drinking and using drugs is fun, and a lot of kids only care about that part of it. But it is also dangerous and illegal. I want you to have the courage to be your own person and to do the right thing even when it isn't popular. Does that make sense?

Q. *What should I do if I'm at a party and there is drinking or drug use going on?*

A. Call us to come get you, or if you are driving, leave immediately. You won't get in trouble. In fact, we will be proud of your good judgment.

Q. *What should I do if someone I am driving with has been drinking or using drugs?*

A. Attempt to get that person to stop driving and call us for a ride home. You might save his life as well as your own. If the driver refuses, ask him to let you out at a safe place, like a restaurant or gas station. Then call us and we'll come get you. You won't get in any trouble. And by the way, if *you* are that driver and have been drinking or using drugs, you can call us for a ride home, also. Again, you won't be punished, because we'd rather have you alive than so afraid of getting into trouble that you kill yourself or someone else.

Q. *What should I say if I'm offered alcohol or other drugs?*

A. I know that it's important for teenagers to be able to say no without looking foolish. Let's talk about some ways that you'd feel comfortable saying no. For example:

- Use humor: "No, thanks, I'm not nearly as dumb as I look."

  "Maybe next life. I'm having too much fun to ruin this one."

  "I would, but that beer just doesn't go with my outfit."

- Ask a question: "Why would I want to do something illegal and that's bad for me?"

  "You know, if everybody is doing something, how cool could it be?"

- Change the subject: "No, thanks. Have you seen that guy who just moved in next to Kim? He's so cool."

- Play it straight: "No, thanks. I'm not into that."

  "That's not smart, man. You can get into a lot of trouble, plus wreck your health."

And whatever you say, it's usually a good idea to start walking away from the trouble. In fact, "walk and talk" is a good motto for avoiding trouble. Now tell me, which of these methods makes the most sense to you? What would you be comfortable saying? (After talking about which refusal lines your child or teen feels most comfortable with, it's a good idea to practice role-playing them. You can play another teen who offers alcohol or drugs to your teen. Then let her practice saying no using the "walk and talk" method.)

Q. *Did you drink before you were legal or use illegal drugs?*

Your answer depends on what you did, but the guideline is the one we discussed in chapter One: tell the truth, but not necessarily the whole truth. If you lie and your child finds out later through a friend or relative, you have shot your credibility. Plus, lying to kids gives them the perceived right to lie to us in return. It is better to tell the truth, focusing on the lessons that you learned and other circumstances. For example:

A.1. I waited until I was legal age to try beer and wine. I was never a binge drinker, because I always felt it was too dangerous to be that out of control. I did experiment with some illegal drugs to see what they were like, and looking back I can see what a foolish risk I was taking. I mean you can never be sure what is in an illegal drug. Plus the drugs available today are more powerful and more dangerous. That's why I hope you will never even try them.

A.2. Too be perfectly honest with you, I wasn't too smart about that stuff when I was a teenager. We were into a lot of stuff that was much too dangerous to be playing around with. I was lucky, but some of the kids I knew weren't. Some became addicts and really messed up their lives, and one even overdosed and died. I can tell you, it isn't worth it. Please, don't ever go down that slippery road. You can slide too far too fast and not recover.

Q. *Why does Grandpa drink so much? (Child)*

A. You noticed that, huh? You are very observant. Well, we think he may have a drinking problem, something called alcoholism. That's when your body wants more and more alcohol and you have trouble stopping. It is a very dangerous disease, because it can hurt your body and cause you not to think straight. We are going to talk to Grandpa about it and try to get him some help.

Q. *Well, is it ever okay to drink? (Child)*

A. Most people can drink when they become adults if they only drink a little at a time, say one or two drinks in a day. But people who are alcoholics should not drink at all, because they have trouble stopping at one or two drinks. Some people also choose not to drink at all because they feel healthier without alcohol or for religious reasons.

Q. *If drugs are bad, why do you give me pills when I'm sick? (Child)*

A. Some drugs are helpful. The ones the doctor prescribes for you when you get sick can help you get well again. We don't take drugs too often, only when they are really needed and then only ones that are legal to take. The bad drugs are those that are not legal to buy. They can make you feel good at first, but can make you sick or even kill you later. You should never take these kinds of drugs, only the ones that Mommy or Daddy say are okay.

Q. *Why do I have to take this stupid drug test?*

A. Because we found this marijuana in your room. You know we have a policy of no illegal drug use in our family and you broke that policy, so now we can't trust you. The only way for us to know that you are not using is to give you random drug tests. If you stay clean for a good while and don't lie to us then you can earn our trust back.

How to Tell if Your Teen Is Using Alcohol or Other Drugs

The best way to monitor your teen's potential use of alcohol or other drugs is be awake when he comes home at night. Glassy eyes, slurred speech, difficulty walking, the smell of alcohol or breath freshener, dilated pupils, or unusual behavior are all signs of use. However, they are not conclusive. Do you also notice dropping grades, a hostile or depressed attitude, heavy identification with the drug culture, a decrease in care about personal appearance or other negative changes? These signs also suggest the possibility of use. Of course, the surest sign that your teen is using is finding alcohol, drugs, or related paraphernalia in his belongings. This is almost always conclusive. Even so, if you find such evidence and confront your teen, expect him to lie. The reason is that for almost all teens a decision to use alcohol or other illegal drugs is also a decision to lie. For this reason, if you see a number of the soft signs of use mentioned above, you may want to search your teen's room looking for the hard evidence you will need in order to have an effective confrontation. While we do not recommend searching a teen's room routinely, if you have sufficient cause to believe that your teen is using, then searching is in order. As an alternative, you might consider a home drug test that you can administer to your teen to see if he has any signs of drugs in his urine. What do you tell your teen before such a severe invasion of his privacy? Anything that you say will probably trigger anger. If he is not using, he may be angry that you do not trust him. If he is using, he will become angry and say that you don't trust him. Either way, be prepared to remain firm yet kind and stand your ground. If you have a partner, talk it over first and decide what you will say. Then confront your teen together. You might say something like this:

"Your father and I have been very concerned about you lately. You get angry easily; you don't seem concerned that your grades are dropping; you look more and more disheveled in your appearance, and when you came home last night your eyes were glassy and you staggered up to bed. We love you and want you to stay healthy, but we are afraid that you might be using alcohol or other drugs. You know how serious we feel kids using drugs is, so you can understand our concern. We don't want to put you in a position where you might be tempted to lie to us, so we thought the best way to see what's going on is for us to do a drug test. Please take this into the bathroom and bring us back a sample of urine. We'll do the test together. Then we'll see what we can do together to understand what's been bothering you."

If your teen refuses, assume that he is using and get help. If the test shows positive, get help. In either case, do not blow up and make the problem worse. Stay calm and loving, but firmly insist that you get help. Even if he is only experimenting and is not a regular user yet, your insistence that you get help sends a message about how important you take this issue. See the list of resources at the back of the book for where to get such help.

You will also want to follow-up on your previous discussions with logically connected consequences for his breaking the rule against using. These might include having to stay home more often, loss of the use of the car for a period, and random drug testing until he begins to earn back your trust. We would also suggest that he be given a research assignment to write an essay about the harmful effects of whatever he is using. Help him go online or to the library and become an expert on why what he has put into his body is such a bad idea.

A Brief Review

The prevalence of alcohol and drug use among teens in our society makes every child at risk. Addiction, impaired judgment, a criminal record, and interference with normal growth and development are all reasons that kids should not use alcohol until they are of legal age and illegal drugs at all. Letting your kids know that you strongly object to their use while talking persuasively about the negative effects of using can help you keep them drug free. Getting through to your kids about this critical topic means getting informed yourself on the effects various drugs have on growing children and teens. Learn their common names and which are most popular now. Find recent statistics to help you build your case when talking to your kids. The Web sites and other resources located in the Resources section can help you easily become well informed on a subject that can have life-and-death consequences for you and your children.

Chapter 5

Courage and Fear . . .
a delicate balance

Four-year-old Terrance walks down a strange hallway, dimly lit and filled with ghostly shadows. His heart pounds in his chest. He looks for his mother, but she is nowhere to be found. At the end of the hall is a door. He is drawn toward it with a dread that he does not understand. His feet move him silently forward. His hand reaches out. Terrance turns the knob and pushes. He is there! The bad man with the sharp teeth! It was a trap! He turns and runs back down the hall and out the front door into the yard! But the bad man is right behind him, running faster. He can feel his breath on his neck. The bad man reaches out and grabs his shoulder. He feels suddenly hot all over. "Don't! Don't!" he screams aloud, and in so doing wakens from the nightmare in a wet sweat. "It's all right, honey," his mother says, her hand on his shoulder. "It was only a dream."

Fourteen-year-old Carla looks suspiciously at the marijuana. "Finally," she thinks, unconcerned and unafraid of any pending consequences, "I've always wanted to know what this stuff feels like." She takes a puff. *Hmm*, she thinks. *Not bad*. She takes another puff, then passes it to her friend Tanya. Tanya's heart is in her throat. A wave of anxiety flows through her stomach and up her chest. She has heard how bad marijuana can be for you, that it can get you suspended from school and in trouble with your parents. She wants no part of it, but she has another, perhaps greater fear. "What will the other kids think of me if I *don't* try it? Will they think I'm a baby or that I'm not cool?" Her twin fears fight for control as the moment stretches into an eternity.

Eight-year-old Darren has practiced throwing and hitting with his dad for hours, and he has improved his baseball playing greatly since last season. But he still remembers what it was like being the worst player on his team, and his stomach is filled with butterflies as he waits for them to call his number for his turn to try out. What if he doesn't hit the ball or misses every chance to catch and throw? All the other kids will be watching. Maybe he should just quit now and avoid the humiliation of failure. He could always get one of his famous stomachaches. That would get him out of it with no major embarrassment. But he really did want to play and he was a lot better this year. "Just keep your eye on the ball and swing hard," his dad had told him. "And if you miss it, you miss it. It's not the end of the world. It's like they said in that movie *Sounder*: 'You get some of what you try for; you don't get any of what you don't try for.' "

What Parents Need to Know

Courage and fear are the twin problems of childhood. And because we each carry the child we were inside our adult minds, it stays with us to some extent our entire lives. Like the poem says, courage is there to urge us on, while fear tries to hold us back. Courage is the positive voice that tells us we can do it while fear tells us that we will fail or get hurt if we try. *Courage*, from the French word *coeur*, meaning "heart," is what Winston Churchill once called "the first and foremost of all qualities, because it is the one upon which all others depend." In fact, without the courage to take a risk, a child cannot develop responsibility, cooperation, intellect, friendship, or even love. All require risk and have a potential for harm.

The mistake we often make, however, is to assume that just because courage is such an overwhelmingly positive trait that fear must be the opposite, a negative trait so despicable that it should be wiped off the planet if at all possible. The truth is that fear is just as valuable to our survival and development as courage. Fear is an emotional warning system that sounds the alarm when we are in a situation that could result in loss. This might be loss of life and limb, money, property, self-esteem, or even control. Without this warning system children would routinely stumble off heights, burn themselves, crash their bikes and other wheeled toys, and otherwise be regulars at the local emergency room if they survived childhood at all. If you know a child who "has no fear," then you immediately recognize this as true. However, if you have a child who is often afraid to try new things or take a risk, you may not appreciate the natural wisdom that this child brings to the table.

As with most things in life, the problem is one of balance. A certain amount of fear is often as useful as a certain amount of courage. Too little fear can lead to foolish risk taking. The teenager in the preceding vignette who gave no thought to the risks of using marijuana could have used more fear. When Princess Diana raced through that fatal tunnel at high speed, perhaps more fear would have helped her tell the driver to slow down, or at least prompted her to buckle her seat belt. When John Kennedy rode fearlessly through the streets of Dallas without the bubble top that the Secret Service wanted him to have, maybe more fear would have saved his life. When his son John

Kennedy, Jr. flew a plane at night into the ocean, killing himself and two others, a healthy fear of night flying and his own inexperience may have made the difference.

Why does fear get such a bad rap when it is obviously here for a useful purpose? The reason is probably that we all have witnessed how excessive fear breeds a life of regret and missed opportunities. Without the courage to face a risk, childhood becomes an endless series of fearful experiences and reduced self-esteem. Kids who become discouraged, who constantly give in to their fears, are not safe and happy. They are safe and miserable. Had the boy in the baseball-tryout vignette given in to his fear and faked a stomachache to avoid possible embarrassment, he would have paid such a price later.

Helping our kids learn to deal with the challenges of life with a healthy balance between courage and fear gives them a foundation of both safety and growth. Some children are naturally cautious or fearful. Others become that way because of life experiences, especially trauma such as natural disasters, violent crime, abuse, war, or disease. Building courage in these children is a gradual process that takes knowledge, patience, and, sometimes, professional help. On the other hand, kids who are naturally fearless risk takers have to be slowed down so that their courage is tempered with a knowledgeable weighing of the risks and rewards. These kids are the proverbial "accidents waiting to happen." Their courage easily becomes recklessness without someone helping them to learn the important counterbalance of fear.

Another reason that fear is so often denigrated is that childhood is a time of many normal fears. We all have painful memories of nightmares, bullies, or other fear-producing events, so it is easy to fall into a "fear is bad" frame of mind. It may be better, however, to think of these normal childhood fears as a way that has evolved for children to learn how to build the delicate balance between courage and fear. These fears help keep children safe while at the same time offering them opportunities to build courage in small, safe ways as they overcome them one by one.

According to researchers Robert Schachter and Carole Spearin McCauley, some of the more typical fears that occur at various ages include: Age one: separation anxiety (fear of leaving a parent), noises, falling, animals, baths, and doctors. Age two: separation anxiety, inconsistent discipline, toilet training, baths, bedtime, and doctors. Age three: animals, toilet training, bedtime, monsters and ghosts, bed wetting, and crippled people. Age four sees some of the others plus loss of a parent and death. Age five: some of the others plus getting lost, going to day care, loss of parent, death, and injury. Ages five to ten: Some of the early childhood fears linger, but as others drop off the list, new ones emerge, such as being late to school, social rejection, criticism, new situations, adoption, burglars, divorce, personal danger, and war. Age ten to sixteen sees the addition of kidnapping, being alone in the dark, injections, heights, terrorism, plane or car crashes, sexual relations, drug use, public speaking, school performance, crowds, and gossip.

If your reaction to this listing of fears is "Wow! What a bunch of chickens we humans are!" remember that all children do not possess all of these fears. In addition, there are degrees of fear from very mild to paralyzing. Chances are that your children will exhibit some of these fears, and that's great. It gives you a chance to build their courage while teaching them to differentiate rational from irrational fear. Consider that courage is not the absence of fear; it is the confidence to overcome fear. We want to teach our children to listen to their fear, even to make friends with it, and then to evaluate what action to take. Sometimes taking action in the face of fear and potential harm or failure is the right thing to do and requires a lot of courage. For that reason, we want to always be building their courage through the process of encouragement.

Tips for Building Courage

Because courage is the foundation for positive action, use these tips to get through to your child, building the confidence to take good risks when the situation calls for it:

1. **Acknowledge strengths**. All children possess strengths in multiple areas. Learn to notice your child's successes and acknowledge them. Use a lot of "attagirl," "attaboy," and "good job" to encourage progress.

2. **Build on strengths.** When your child is too afraid to take a positive action in one step, find a success that you can build upon. For example, if your six-year-old is afraid to swim across the pool, acknowledge how well he did swimming across the shallow end. Then find an intermediate step that is within his comfort range. For example, maybe he will swim the length of the pool if you swim beside him.

3. **Praise the effort, not just the result.** Courage does not imply always succeeding. When a child has the courage to risk failure and then fails, let her know how proud you are of her effort.

4. **Show acceptance for your child.** Win or lose, your child needs to know that your love and acceptance for them as your child is not changed. "I couldn't love you any more or be happier to have you as my daughter if you became the first woman presi-

dent" is the kind of attitude that builds a bedrock of courage and self-esteem.

5. **Stimulate independence.** Protecting our children from harm is a cornerstone of parenting. Ironically, *overprotection* can be one of the most handicapping things a parent can do to a child. It robs a child of the courage that comes from struggling through life's problems and finding solutions. Instead, teach your child to become independent. Gradually give him more and more responsibility, keeping it in line with his age and level of maturity. A good rule of thumb is to never do on a regular basis what your child can do for himself.

What Children Need to Know

During early childhood, many of our fears are irrational in the sense that there is no reasonable danger of which to be afraid. For example, the nightmare of "the bad man with the sharp teeth" at the beginning of the chapter is an irrational fear. The man cannot possibly hurt the child, because he isn't real. He is just a bad dream. But to a fear-soaked four-year-old, he seems very real, even after the child wakes up. While an older child or an adult might be relieved to wake up from a nightmare to discover that it was "just a dream," a young child often cannot differentiate between the real and the unreal. His brain is just not developed enough yet. The wall between fantasy and reality is still too tenuous. Telling him that there is nothing to be afraid of is not likely to help. In fact, it may just destroy your credibility, since he *knows* full well that there is something very much to be afraid of.

A better approach is to start with empathy. For example, "You had a bad dream. That can be very scary." Acknowledging the fear, while labeling it for what it is, "a bad dream," offers the child an ally ("she understands and seems to take me seriously—so I'm not alone in this fight") while setting the stage for him to begin understanding rational from irrational fears when he is ready ("I don't know what a bad dream is, but Mom doesn't seem too upset by it, not like she was when I ran out into the street and she ran out to grab me, so maybe it will be okay").

This same empathy is important with all fears, rational or irrational, from early childhood through the late teen years and into adulthood. How many adults get weak-kneed with fear at the thought of making a public speech? The answer is millions since public speaking is the number one fear for adults in our society. The fact that there are hundreds more lethal things in our lives that would be more rational to fear suggests that fear is often irrationally based for all of us. Therefore, telling a child that "there is nothing to be afraid of" is not only unlikely to help but will probably be heard as an insult and make your further opinions on the subject unwelcome.

Once you have offered empathy and established yourself as an ally, then we suggest going back to step one and asking good questions. This can help in a number of ways. First, asking questions engages the intellectual aspects of the brain, pulling it away from the emotional areas where fear resides. When your child is thinking analytically about your questions, she is less focused on the fear. Second, good questions can help you both see areas where irrational beliefs are perpetuating the fear. Take for example the girl in the opening vignette who was afraid of smoking marijuana *and* afraid of losing her friends. If she were to confide this dilemma to her parents through some good questioning (as well as an extremely high degree of trust and respect), it might uncover an irrational belief that she needs to be liked by *these* girls. This is not an uncommon belief among teenagers, just an irrational one. It gives the parent a good opportunity to move into Step 2 and give her opinions persuasively. In this case she may want to help her daughter understand that although we each need friends, we do not need any *particular* friends. What is more important is too find good friends, people who share many of your values and whom you can count on to be supportive and encouraging. Kids who entice you to use drugs or other harmful activities do not make the best friends, no matter how cool they seem or how much fun they are to be around. Her daughter's fear of rejection by these kids will be diminished if she accepts the belief that she can make other, better friends.

Some Good Questions to Ask When Your Child Is Afraid

1. **Can you tell me what happened?** Whether a bad dream or a conflict with friends, it helps both parties to tell the story out loud. Sharing with an ally what happened that triggered the fear can often help to diminish the fear by itself. In addition, it gives the parent useful information from which to ask further questions or to provide persuasive information.

2. **What's the worst thing that could happen?** This question may seem counterproductive at first thought. However, a child's emotional fear response is often out of proportion with the reality of the situation. Helping a child think about the worst-case scenario can help him put the situation into perspective and reduce the fear. Of course, if the worst that could happen is unreasonably dangerous, then perhaps the child should listen to the fear and turn back.

3. **Is your fear helping you or hurting you this time?** This question builds on the notion that fear can be for better or for worse. Teaching our children to listen to their fears and then decide what action to take is a lifelong lesson in risk management.

4. **What might you do to improve the situation?** Action is the best antidote for fear. Any athlete will tell you that sitting around waiting for the big game to begin or your turn to play is the most anxiety provoking. Once the game has begun, you are too active to be bothered by fear. The emotional energy that was fear has become the motivational energy to succeed. Similarly, when we get through to our children to take some positive action in times of fear, we help them cope. The child who is afraid of the bad man with the sharp teeth might take a flashlight and go with the parent around the house checking to make sure that there are no lurkers. This can also be effective with a ten-year-old who hears a noise at night and needs reassurance that there are no intruders. The fourteen-year-old who is afraid of having no friends can be encouraged to invite someone new over to spend the night or go to an activity.

Persuading Kids to Give up Irrational Fears

If action is the antidote to fear, then words alone will rarely be successful in helping a child give up an irrational fear. Still, helping a child change some of his mistaken beliefs can provide the courage to take the positive action that can prove "my fears won't stop me." For example, if your child has an excessive fear of dogs, you might begin by telling her something like:

"You are perfectly right to be afraid of *some dogs*. It can be dangerous to approach strange dogs, and your fear is smart to tell you to be careful. But most dogs are friendly and can be a lot of fun to play with. We have to teach your fear not to get in the way of your playing with *those* dogs. Would you like that?"

You will want to assure her that she will not have to be around a dog until she is ready and that you will take it as slowly as she wants. It is never a good idea to overwhelm a child with fear in an attempt to get them over it. Making her pet a dog, even a friendly one, can easily backfire and cause much more harm than good.

Stephen and Marianne Garber and Robyn Spizman, in their book *Monsters Under the Bed and Other Childhood Fears*, suggest a gradual approach to eliminating fears:

1. Find out exactly what your child is afraid of. Is she afraid of all dogs or just a type of dog or a color or size of dog?

2. Find a way to quantify how afraid she is. This might be a ten point scale or have her let you know how "full" of fear she is: "up to your knees or up to your waist . . . over your head."

3. Find a first step that your child can tolerate as a place to begin. Maybe she can look at a picture of a friendly dog and only feel fear up to her knees, for example. Look at the picture together and talk about some of the positive aspects of the dog. Help her understand how to treat dogs and take care of them.

4. Find a book about a dog or maybe a video with a dog hero. Watch it together and then talk about how she felt.

5. Work up to seeing a friendly dog from a distance playing with other children. Do not push her to interact, but talk about what she sees and feels. When she feels only little or no fear,

you can take her closer. Encourage how well she is doing and point out her progress. Remind her that you are taking it as slowly as she needs to take it. Taking deep breaths is also helpful, as it tends to relax a child. So remind her to breathe deeply when she begins to feel the fear.

6. Eventually have her pet the dog.

Persuading Kids to Be More Cautious

With children and teens who have low degrees of fear and are constantly getting hurt or into trouble, your goal is help them slow their engines and become more cautious. Getting through to them about the advantages of caution is an ongoing process that will proceed in baby steps. Do not become discouraged yourself if such kids seem to agree with you, but then go right back to their impulsive behavior. It takes a lot of work and frequent reminders to help some kids learn to become more reflective in their decision-making. For other kids, it also takes medication. If you suspect that your child has ADHD (attention deficit hyperactivity disorder), then you will want to get him evaluated by a specialist and consider the possibility of a medication trial. For all kids, however, the following tips can help you teach them to "look before you leap."

TIPS FOR HELPING KIDS BECOME MORE CAUTIOUS

1. **Talk about the need to think first, act second.** Talk to your kids about the difference between thinking and doing. Impulsive, high-risk takers have very little space between the two. Your

job is to help them increase this space so that they have time to reflect about the possible dangers of an action.

2. **Count to ten and take a deep breath.** Teach your child to count to ten when she is faced with a choice and to breath deeply. This has the effect of slowing a person down and calming him slightly.

3. **Name the risks.** Helping a child recognize and name the risks involved with a course of action helps get through to her control center. The naming of the risk, either out loud or to themselves, has the effect of breaking through the tendency to deny risk and plunge ahead. For example, the teen in the opening vignette with no fear of marijuana can be taught to stop and say to herself such things as: "I could get into a lot of trouble for this; I could mess up my thinking; this stuff could be laced with something more dangerous, even deadly; I would be letting my parents down."

4. **Look for a good metaphor.** Since slowing a high-risk taker down is an ongoing process, finding a good metaphor can give you a shorthand way of getting through. For example, if your child is a golfer, you might say: "When Tiger Woods is up at the tee he doesn't just go up to the ball and cream it. He first looks over the hole and notices where the trouble is. He might see a water hazard over to the right and think, 'Hmm, there is no need to hit it over there and risk losing a stroke. There isn't enough to gain by taking that chance. It's a smarter and safer play to keep it left where the fairway is broader.' I want you to be like Tiger in that way every time you face a decision. Think about where the hazards are before you swing and stay out of

the water." Later, when your child faces a decision, you can capture the entire message again by just saying, "Do you see any water hazards, Tiger?"

5. **Look for alternatives and evaluate consequences.** Talk with your child about problems that come up in her life using active listening and lots of empathy. Then help your child think critically about alternatives for handling the problem. After each alternative ask, "What do you think would happen if you tried that?" Continue helping her think about the likely consequences of various actions until she finds one that seems acceptable. This analytical exercise will help your child learn that there are more ways to skin a cat than her first impulse.

6. **Teach him to consider others.** When talking about the consequences of a potential action with your child, be sure to ask the question "How will this affect others?" This not only teaches the invaluable skill of empathy, but will also make some kids who have little fear for their own sake take a less risky course of action for the sake of others.

QUESTIONS KIDS SOMETIMES ASK (AND POSSIBLE ANSWERS)

The following questions and answers will serve to get you thinking about some of the common fears of childhood. How you answer will be dictated by your understanding of your own child and the circumstance within which you live.

Q. *Could someone break into our house?*

A. It is scary to think about someone breaking into our house. But it is good that you are cautious, because although it is unlikely to happen, it can happen. What do you think that we can do to make our house as safe as possible? Do you want to go around with me and check that all the windows and doors are locked? If we did find that someone had broken into our house, what would we do?

Q. *Will our country be bombed?*

A.1. War is a terrible thing, and I can understand why you'd be concerned.

A.2. It is scary for all of us right now. So far we haven't been bombed, but with all the fighting, it is possible. This is why our military is fighting to keep us safe. What else can you think of that will help us stay safe?

Q. *Will our airplane crash?*

A. It's a funny thing about airplanes, they almost never crash. But when they do they make big news, so a lot of people are more scared to fly than they need to be. In fact, ever since the terrorist attacks flying is still a lot safer than driving. Plus, they've added a lot of security to make it even safer. It's okay to be a little nervous, though. Do you want to do something together to take your mind off of it? What about reading a book with me?

Q. *What do I do if I get lost at the mall?*

A. Good question. It's always smart to anticipate problems just in case. We need to try to stay together, but if you do get separated, go right to one of the people working the cash register at the store, or go into a store and find the person working at the cash register. Tell that person that you are lost and ask them to help. They will get someone to help find me. (Or if you have a cell phone . . .) Ask them to call me on my cell phone. What's the number to call?

Q. *Could you get cancer?*

A. I suppose I could. Anybody can get a disease like cancer. I take good care of myself, though, and I certainly don't plan on getting cancer or any other serious disease. What has you thinking about cancer, though? Did you hear about someone getting it?

Q. *Could I get kidnapped?*

A. I'm glad you're thinking about your safety. Kidnapping doesn't happen very often. In fact, you'll probably never even know someone who gets kidnapped. But because it does happen sometimes, we have to be careful. Let's talk about some of the ways that you can make sure you never get kidnapped. What do you remember about talking or going with strangers? What if they tell you that I was in an accident and they were sent to come get you? What if they tell you that they are making a movie and they want you to be in it? What if you are playing in the yard and they drive up and ask you for directions?

Q. *Will you ever leave me?*

A Not in a million zillion trillion years. But someday you will leave me. But not until you're all grown up and ready to be on your own.

A Brief Review

Courage and fear are twin challenges that every child has to face. When handled effectively, courage provides the confidence to take risks that are necessary to grow and develop, while fear slows kids down and provides a warning system for determining when risks might be too dangerous. Parents can help get through to kids about how to manage the normal and often irrational risks of childhood while building courage and self-esteem in the process. The result is a healthy balance between the two and a decision-making process that considers both the risks and the rewards.

In times of crisis such as economic depression, war or the challenge of terrorism, parents too may also struggle with the balance between courage and fear. Is it really safe to fly? Should we avoid shopping malls and other places where large numbers of people gather? Is it even safe to open our mail for fear of anthrax or some other biological agent? Such questions need rational answers. As parents it is our job to get these answers calmly and with a confidence that lets our children know that they are in good hands. While anthrax, as most of us have learned, is not contagious, fear is. And kids can catch it from their parents. When parents panic and become afraid to take even reasonable risks such as flying and going out in public, it sends a message to their children to be even more afraid.

Talk with other parents. Listen to experts. Find out what is a reasonable risk and what is a foolish one. If need be, seek professional counseling to help regain your own balance. Most people have more courage than they realize and challenging times can provide the motivation to dig deep inside to find the reservoir of courage that is there. Human growth seldom comes in times of tranquillity. It is the crisis that offers us that opportunity.

Chapter 6

Death . . .
the ultimate price of life

They stood alone in front of the open casket, mother and son gazing in awe at the lifeless body of their father and grandfather. The fragrant scent of flowers, the quiet talking of friends and relatives in the background, the smooth hardwood and satin lining of his final resting place all seemed to blur under the enormity of the occasion. Eight-year-old Ben spoke first. "He doesn't look like Grandpa very much."

"No," his mother replied. "All his wonderful expression is gone from his face."

"He looks like he is asleep or something," added Ben.

"Death looks a little like sleep, but it's much different. You wake up from sleep. Death is forever."

"Why do people die?" asked her son.

"Death is part of life. Everything that lives must die. It's part of the plan."

"Why must everything die?" he asked, not accepting her answer.

"That's the way God made things."

"Why did God make things like that?"

"I've wondered that myself. I don't know for sure, but maybe it was to make life special. If life lasted forever, it wouldn't be nearly as special. It's knowing that we only have a certain amount of time that makes every day such a precious gift. Grandpa knew this and lived a very full and happy life. We can be happy for him."

"Then why are you crying, Mommy?"

"Because I loved him. And when somebody you love dies, you miss him. I miss Grandpa. But I have lots of special memories of him in my heart, and those good memories will make me feel better soon."

"I miss Grandpa, too."

What Parents Need to Know

We expect grandparents to die, and so we are somewhat prepared when they do. But did you know that in the United States alone, one in twenty children under the age of eighteen will experience the death of a parent. In one study, 19 percent of these children showed serious problems at one year and 21 percent at two years. Millions of other children will experience the loss of other close friends and relatives, plus the protracted illnesses of themselves and/or others. In addition, with today's ubiquitous media reporting live camera coverage of such historical tragedies as the space shuttle *Challenger* explosion, the O. J. Simpson murder trial, and the Columbine High School massacre, it is unlikely that any child will grow up without at least a vicarious experience of a significant death. The innocence of childhood is yet another fatality of our brief moment in history. All children now need to be prepared to deal with the fundamental issues of life and death in psychologically healthy ways.

Death has awed and mystified humankind since the beginning of our history. We recognize it as an integral and inevitable part of life, yet we hunger for answers that will make its finality somehow acceptable. At times we face death courageously with firmness and resolution. At times we stand trembling in the dark like a frightened child who has just wakened from a nightmare, unsure of what is real and what is a dream. We marshal our coping skills creatively in the form of philosophy, science, psychology, and perhaps especially, religion, in an attempt to come to terms with the mortality of our species. And yet until we have looked into the eyes of our own inevitable deaths and, unblinking, accepted this strange and complex aspect of life, we cannot fully experience our own lives, let alone help our children make the most of theirs.

Perhaps you have answered the questions of mortality to your own satisfaction. Perhaps you continue to struggle. Perhaps you believe that dead is dead and that's the end of it. Maybe you believe in heaven or some other afterlife, and that a deceased loved one is "in a better place." Maybe your faith tells you that the spirit is reincarnated and given another opportunity to apply the lessons of the previous life. Whatever your belief, you will want to share it with your children as a way of helping them gain comfort and understanding. Yet, we encourage you to leave room for your child to struggle with the questions herself, so that her own mind is strengthened in the process. Know that she may not come to the same conclusions as you. After all, where death is concerned, there seem to be many different yet helpful answers chosen by people who have lived worthwhile, successful lives in countries around the world.

One value does seem to be universal: Life is good. Helping our children appreciate the gift of life and all that it offers is one cornerstone of death education. The mother in the opening vignette used the circumstance of her father's funeral to help her son appreciate just how special life is. Death makes life valuable. It also presents a time limit, which acts as a great motivator for action. People are such procrastinators that without death to motivate us, we'd never get around to doing anything! On a more scientific level, death is a necessary ingredient for evolution. It allows room for the gene pool to mutate into higher forms of life. Plus, without death, can you imagine the overpopulation problem? How would you like to compete with a billion other humans for a parking place?

The fact that life is good does not mean that death is necessarily a bad thing. However, it is a painful thing. Fully functioning human beings form attachments to people they care about and are able to empathize with those they do not even know. When we lose somebody to death we experience a loss that sends pain throughout our minds and bodies. Healing from this loss takes time. It is a matter of grief work and can be facilitated with the support of loved ones, knowledge of the process, and positive thoughts and actions.

A Child's Grief Is a Gift

Because loving parents do not like to see their children in pain, they often take steps to shield them from grief. This is a mistake that can cause more pain later in many less obvious ways. For example, a child who is told not be sad about his mother's death because "she is in a better place," may deny her sadness until it emerges later in the form of somatic symptoms such as stomachaches, behavioral problems, or depression. Parents who leave their children out of the discussions and rituals surrounding death may actually create more anxiety as the children are left wondering what is going on and feeling very alone.

Certainly we want to be gentle in helping our children deal with serious illness and death. We do not want to introduce new trauma by scaring them. For example, forcing a child to view the open casket of a deceased person when he is obviously afraid and protesting can do damage and should be avoided. However, the grief process itself is a gift that can strengthen the child emotionally while bringing the psychological closure needed to put the loss experience in the past. This can't be done by simply telling a child to "move on with your life." It requires support, talk, action, pain, and time. Do not try to rush the process. Your child's pain now will become emotional muscle later. Talking honestly and compassionately about illness and death with your child can help you turn the experience into a gift of insight and wisdom that will enrich his life forever.

Children Are Different From You and Me

No two people grieve in exactly the same way. However, there are enough similarities that some common stages of grief have emerged in the literature. We discussed these stages in chapter 8 on Divorce (see pages 99–113). We described how people need to move through three broad stages of shock, suffering, and acceptance. Although children have much in common with adults concerning loss and grief, the differences are important to keep in mind.

Young children (those under the age of five) will not usually grasp the concept of death. They experience it as separation, and even an infant can feel the pain of being separated from a caregiver with whom he has attached. Because they lack the necessary abstract thinking, they may think of death as temporary or reversible, as they see in cartoons. They may believe that they can wish the person alive again. Sometimes a young child will mistakenly believe that someone's death is a punishment for something the child has done wrong. Often it takes time before a young child even comprehends that the loved one is really gone.

Gently correct their misconceptions and reassure them that they are not to blame. Let them know that you are there for them and that they will always be cared for. Because young children think very concretely, avoid euphemisms such as "going to sleep" (which may lead to sleeping problems) or "passed away" (which has little meaning for a child). Instead, use concrete language, such as "Death means a person's body has stopped working forever and that they will no longer be with us." Be patient as young children often ask the same questions over and over again as their minds absorb more information each time. Although funeral services may be too traumatic for young children, you can find other ways to help them commemorate the loss of a loved one, such as drawing pictures or planting a memorial tree.

After about age six children are able to understand that death is permanent and inevitable. They can grasp the fact of their own mortality, which can sometimes create a fear of death, particularly after a traumatic experience such as a murder or accident. Like younger children, older children will often act out their grief through displays of emotion. Parents can encourage them to name their feelings, helping to put their grief into words such as anger, sadness, hurt, and guilt. Children this age can be offered the opportunity to go to the hospital to visit, view the body, and attend the funeral or memorial service. Respect their wishes and do not force a child to participate if she refuses. Look for other ways to help the child memorialize the loved one. You will also want to maintain as normal a routine as possible, including discipline.

Children will sometimes cope with the shock of a painful death by regressing to an earlier stage of development. For example, a six-year-old may begin wetting the bed and a four-year-old might start sucking his thumb again. Do not discipline such regressive behaviors. As children move through the stages of grief, they will usually give them up on their own, or with some gentle encouragement.

Teenagers can take understanding death to another level as they attempt to integrate the concept into a developing philosophy of life. They may seem depressed as they grapple with questions about the meaning of life and "Who am I?" Talking with them about their feelings and helping them think about illness and death can help teens heal from the experience and find meaning in the process. Encourage them to help in planning the funeral or memorial, and to think of creative ways to say goodbye. For example, some teenage friends of a suicide victim built a gazebo to commemorate their friend's life. As with all children, productive action is often a useful way to alleviate negative emotions and move toward letting go.

Sometimes children experience what is called "complicated grief." In such instances, children seem stuck in their grief and are unable to resume normal activities. Regressive behavior may continue, as well as deep sadness, anger, or fear. Complicated grief is more likely to occur with a sudden or traumatic death; when there are multiple losses; when a child has been neglected or abused before the death; when a social stigma is attached, such as suicide or homicide; or when the surviving parent is unable to grieve. Although it is difficult to set a time limit for normal grief, as sadness will often linger intermittently for years, a good rule of thumb is that if a child is not resuming normal behavior and activities within six months, the grief is complicated, and a professional counselor or psychologist should be consulted.

TIPS FOR HELPING CHILDREN DEAL WITH ILLNESS AND DEATH

1. **Prepare them.** A child can learn about death from watching television, going to movies, or reading stories. Talk with them about what they watch and read, helping them to make sense of illness and death while encouraging your own family values. These vicarious experiences of death can help prepare them for personal experiences. The first of these personal experiences often comes with the death of a pet. From goldfish and turtles to the intimate relationship that a child can have with a dog or a cat, the death of a pet offers a good opportunity to talk about the process of death and the grief that follows loss. In the event that a loved one is critically ill, do not give a child false hope that things are all right. It is better to gently prepare her for the worst by saying that the person is very ill and may not get better. Prepare the child for the separation by letting her visit the hospital to spend time with the loved one.

2. **Include the children.** Children are often called "the forgotten mourners," because adults are often too busy with the added details involved with a loss, as well as their own grief, to pay attention to the children. Make sure that you involve them in the mourning process in ways that are appropriate for their age, making sure to take plenty of time to talk together.

3. **Tell the truth.** Honesty does not have to be brutal, but it may hurt nonetheless. Still, it is the only way to go. If you mislead your child or hide the truth, she will eventually find out and feel hurt *and* deceived. Young children do not need to know all of the details involved with a death. Just give them the

basic information. For example, "Daddy has died. That means his body has stopped working, and he won't be with us anymore. It's very sad and we will miss him a lot." As children get older, they will ask about what they need to know. Answer them honestly, with compassion, giving information that will help them learn from the experience. For example, "Your brother died from an overdose of drugs. We loved him very much and we will all miss him. I hate that he put that stuff in his body, because it is so dangerous."

4. **Use stories and metaphors to get through.** There are many fine books written to communicate with children about illness and death. These books often use animals as main characters, a device particularly useful with children under the age of six. Read these stories together being sure to discuss and apply the lessons to your own situation. Older children and teens can be helped through children's literature that accomplishes the same goals of teaching them how to handle and understand death. Read them aloud together if your child is willing, always taking time to discuss afterward.

5. **Talk about feelings.** It is important for children to learn to express painful feelings such as fear, anger, guilt, and sadness. Young children can be helped by using physical means such as painting, modeling with clay, and using stuffed animals and puppets. They can draw pictures of the deceased or sculpt a bust. You might take two puppets or dolls and tell the child that they have just lost someone they loved. Ask them how they think the dolls feel about their loss—for example, sad or angry. Children and teens need to know that it is okay to feel whatever they are feeling. Keeping a journal or writing a letter to the deceased are ways to help express

these important feelings. Learn to listen for the feelings behind your child's questions and comments, and then suggest a feeling word that applies. For example, "You sound *worried* about Mommy being in the hospital." "I can hear how *sad* you are that Daddy has died." "I don't blame you for being *angry.*"

6. **Use the power of touch.** There is tremendous comforting power in human touch. Just putting your hand on your child's arm or leg while looking into her eyes and sharing your understanding of the feelings she is experiencing can help a child know that she is not alone. Your touch says this much louder than words and says it at a visceral level that is felt throughout the child's being. A long hug or just letting your child lie against your chest while you lovingly stroke his hair can provide a healing that we do not fully understand for children, teens and even adults. If you are not a "touchy-feely" person, we suggest you become one—if not for your own sake, for that of your children. Start with a hand on a shoulder or a simple hug and work at it from there. You'll be surprised how you can learn to break through once you decide to overcome your perceived limitations.

7. **Gently correct mistaken ideas and offer new perspectives.** Children can become stuck in the stages of grief due to mistaken ideas that only serve to generate unrealistic guilt, anger, or hopelessness. Be gentle when confronting these ideas, letting your child know that you love and accept him even when challenging some of his ideas. For example, "Children sometimes misbehave, but that's not why Daddy died. He died because his heart stopped working right. He loved you a lot, and that's always a good thing."

8. **Reassure your child.** Let your child know that you will get through this together. With young children you might make up a rhyme. For example, "It may be hard and it may take time, but pulling together, we'll be fine." Older children and teens need to be reassured, also. "This is a tough time for our family, but we are strong and we will make it through." Children who are grieving may sometimes think the feelings of sadness will last forever. Reassure them that although grief is painful, healing will come and they will return to feeling secure and happy again. Even so, they can expect to feel a tinge of sadness from time to time as they lovingly remember their loved one. This sweet sadness is one way that we stay connected to the beauty of our relationship with the deceased and another way of honoring the person's memory. It often comes back on the anniversary of the death, the person's birthday, or other significant times. Suggest to your child that she learn to treasure these memories when they come, and not fear them.

9. **Get them involved.** Help children work through their grief in action as well as words. From making get-well cards for a sick loved one to creating a memorial to a pet to commemorating the life of a parent through pictures and words, an involved child feels much better than a passive one. And give your child the gift of memories by talking about the deceased and remembering special times and unique aspects of the person. Making a memory album or a video from old tapes of the loved one is not only a great memorial, but helps the child move toward an acceptance of the death.

10. **Get other people involved.** Healing seems to come better when people have compassionate support groups to help. Children are like adults in this. You will want to spend extra

time with your children following a significant death or during an illness. But you are only one person and your time is limited. Reach out to friends and relatives who can include your child in activities and spend quality time with them. Also, notify your child's school and his teacher so that they can be sensitive to his feelings in the days that follow.

QUESTIONS KIDS SOMETIMES ASK (AND POSSIBLE ANSWERS)

Q. *What is death?*
With a young child, a simple concrete answer is best.

A. Death is when the body stops working forever.

Q. *Is Grandpa going to die?*
As always, compassionate honesty is the best policy.

A. Everything that lives is going to die someday. Grandpa is very sick. He is in the hospital so that the doctors and nurses can help him get better. We don't know right now whether he will get well or not. We will have to wait and see.

Q. *Will you die, too?*
A close death will clue kids into the fact that their parents and themselves are not immortal. A matter-of-fact explanation, coupled with reassurance that you will probably not die for a long time, can help. You can also use the opportunity to reinforce the value of a healthy lifestyle.

A. Sure. Everybody dies someday. But I plan to live for a long long time before I do. That's why I take good care of myself. I exercise and watch what I eat. I don't take drugs except for what the doctor orders. I'm careful when I drive. Like I said, I plan to live a long, long time. How about you?

Q. *What happens to you after you die?*

This is another big one that you will want to answer whether asked or not. The answer will, of course, depend on your spiritual beliefs. Although some people are quite certain that their beliefs are facts, and state them as such to their children, others prefer to state beliefs as beliefs. For example:

A. That's a really good question. In fact people have been trying to answer it for as long as humans have been here. Different people believe different things about what happens after death. We believe that after you die . . . (If you do not have a strong belief about this, it is okay to share that with your child. For example:

No one really knows what happens to us after we die, because no one has ever died and come back to tell us. What we do know is that life is precious and that we should use the time we have wisely. We also know that when we die, the people who knew us or our work remember us, and we want to live in a way that people will remember us warmly or with love.

If you believe in an afterlife, sharing this can be a genuine comfort to your child.

Q. *Who will die next?*

This is one of the usually unasked fear-based questions that follow a death in the family. It is especially likely to be thought if there has been more than one death in the family. While you do not want to give false reassurance, you can offer some comfort.

A. I know it feels like death is everywhere sometimes. Grandma Sal died last Christmas and now Uncle Jim has died. Sometimes a family can go a long time without anyone dying, and then sometimes it seems that a lot of people are dying fast. Fortunately, Grandma Sal and Uncle Jim each lived a long, good life, so they had lots of time to do the things they wanted and to be with the people they loved. We never know who will die next, but we can hope that it is somebody who has lived a long time and done a lot with his or her life like Grandma Sal and Uncle Jim.

Q. *What will happen to me if you die?*

Because kids are vulnerable in the world, death often triggers a fear of abandonment. All parents should have a last will and testament made out that clearly determines who the children will live with should both parents die. You do not need to give the details of this to your children in order to reassure them that they will be well taken care of.

A. If I die, then Daddy (Mommy) will still be here to take care of you. It almost never happens that both parents die, but if that were to happen, then you would live with Uncle Ted and Aunt Lisa and your cousins. But like I said, that's not likely to happen. I just want you to know that no matter what happens, there will be people who love you and are there to take care of you.

Q. *What will we do without Mommy?*

When children lose a parent they often wonder how things can possibly go on without the parent there. Your calm reassurance can give them the security needed to cope with the loss.

A. We will miss Mommy very much because we love her very much. But you and I are strong, and we will be able to handle things together.

Q. *Why did she have to die? It isn't fair!*

Children are very attuned to issues of fairness, and untimely deaths seem to them totally unjust. This question is not so much a request for information as it is an expression of anger over the perceived travesty of taking away their loved one. There are many ways to answer the question, but the late author Mary Jo Hanniford, in the book *Windows: Healing and Helping Through Loss,* cautions against telling the child that it is "God's will." This answer can be counterproductive and turn children against God just when a belief in a loving and just God can help the healing process. Instead, speak to the child's emotions. For example:

A. I don't blame you for being angry. It seems so unfair when somebody dies, especially when they are still so young. I wish there were an easy answer to give you, but maybe that's just one of those things that we will never fully know. In the meantime, what I do know is that we were lucky to have known him, and that we can keep his spirit alive in our hearts for as long as we remember him.

A Quick Review

Children are often the forgotten grievers, so it is important to make sure that they are supported in moving through the stages of grief—from shock and suffering to acceptance and healing. We can use our compassion to help them feel understood and supported; our knowledge to help them understand death and feel secure that they will cope and be taken care of; and our encouragement to involve them in actions that can further their healing and add meaning and richness to their lives. For example, helping your child write a letter to the deceased is one way to get through to them about how to cope with their feelings of loss while still preserving the memory of the loved one. A few simple clues can help them with the writing. For example, when writing to a deceased mother:

1. Tell her how you feel.

2. Tell her what special things you remember about her.

3. Tell her something special about what you are doing.

4. Tell her how much you love her.

Dear Mommy,

I miss you. I miss the walks in the woods we used to take before you got sick. I miss the way you put your arm around me while we marched and sang together. I miss the stories you used to read me at bedtime and the way you always tucked me in and kissed me good night. I even miss you reminding me to clean up my room and take a bath.

I am sad that you are gone, but Daddy, Lisa, and I are taking care of ourselves pretty good. Your French toast is better, though. Daddy uses too much milk. We all went to the zoo last weekend. They have a new gorilla whose name is Willie B. Daddy asked us where does a 400-pound gorilla sleep? Anywhere he wants to. Ha-ha.

I love you and miss you a lot. I am making an album of all my favorite pictures of us together. I'll save it and show it to my kids someday, so they won't forget who you are.

Love,
Michael

Chapter 7

Divorce . . .
the big D

Alexandra sat in her window seat and stared at the moon. She wondered if he was looking at the same moon tonight and thinking of her as she was thinking of him. Did he wonder what she looked like and how she was doing in school and who her friends were? Would he remember that she was almost ten now and that ten was a special birthday? It meant that she wasn't a little kid anymore. She was almost into double figures! Ten also meant it had been almost three years since he moved away. He had promised to write as often as he could, but after a few letters, they had stopped without a trace. "Why don't parents keep their promises?" she wondered. The moon seemed sad now, like a big tear had melted across its happy face and made it all wet. She rubbed her eyes. "I wonder if Daddy is sad tonight."

From the child's perspective nothing is more awe-inspiring as those giants of sustenance, power, and love who seem capable of all things great and small—one's parents. No wonder that for centuries humans have referred to God as "Our Father" and nature as

"Mother." Is there anything more divine to the child in all of us than our creators, Mommy and Daddy? No wonder that issues related to parents have filled the chairs of therapists for decades and left the corners of our minds searching for answers to questions barely conscious. Our parents. Love them or hate them, admire them or pity them, there is one undeniable truth: They are a salient part of our history and who we are. And this fact is a hundred times truer for a child.

Separation and divorce hit kids hard—harder than we would like to think. And even though the stigma of being from a "broken home" is no longer a usual problem, the fact is that divorce shatters the child's world and is still a traumatic event that requires effective handling by the parent. Getting through to our kids in such cases is not easy. After all, we are both the medium *and* the message. For example, when a parent talks to a child about divorce, it is not something that is being inflicted upon the child from the outside like a bee sting or a problem at school. It is something that the parent has brought about himself with no consultation from the child. Getting through their disappointment and anger *at us* so that we can help *them* requires patience, skill, and a lot of empathy.

It also may require a lot of courage. Often the parent left to deal with the child on a day-to-day basis is also suffering the trauma of divorce. Dealing with one's own loss and grief while helping a child or children deal with theirs demands a lot from parents at a time when they may not feel that they have much left to give. This is where courage is needed. Human beings have a great capacity to rise to the occasion, especially when the health and safety of their children are at stake. If you are in such a situation, know that you have resources inside yourself that you have not even begun to use yet. Know, too, that you have friends, family, and resources in the community who would love to help if you will ask them.

What Parents Need to Know: Divorce

Most experts agree that divorce is a lot harder on children than we used to believe. Even so-called *good divorces*—ones in which the parents are civil to each other, stay involved in the lives of their children, and even cooperate—leave their mark on the child's developing attitudes and values. This does not mean that parents should never divorce, but with the divorce rate at about 50 percent of all marriages, it probably means that we need to work a lot harder at improving unsatisfying unions rather than just "making a new start" by heading for the hills when the going gets tough.

Having said that, we also believe that if you are divorced or divorcing that you can do a lot to help mitigate the effects of your failure on your children. Perhaps the best thing that you can do is to work out a cooperative relationship with your child's other parent. Ironically, many couples who could not cooperate while together are able to put their children's needs above their own anger and do so for the sake of their children.

Even with a cooperative relationship between parents, divorce represents a major loss for both parents and children, and like any significant loss it carries with it grief. How this grief is experienced is an individualistic experience, and though no two people grieve in exactly the same way, there are some predictable stages that most people seem to move through. The first stage is often characterized by shock and denial. The child may feel numb or perhaps feel as if it all seems unreal—as if she were watching a movie of someone else's life. "This can't be happening to *our* family" is not an uncommon attitude. Sometimes children will deny that they feel any pain and act as if everything is all right. But deep inside, most kids are hurting for the losses that divorce inevitably brings: loss of the intact family, loss of daily time with one parent, loss of security, sometimes loss of lifestyle.

Stage 2 might be called the time of suffering. Kids, and often parents, may feel all types of painful emotions including sadness, hurt, and anger. Although unpleasant to experience, when faced courageously, these feelings can pave the way for real healing and growth. Children and parents need to carry on through this period, going to work and to school, but in quiet moments at home or in the car, experiencing these feelings fully can often help. For children, having a parent listen to their expressions of suffering with empathy and reassurance can help the process along.

Sometimes children get stuck in Stage 2 and carry their pain with them for years. This can be the result of inaccurate beliefs about themselves or the divorce. For example, a child who believes that his bad behavior caused the divorce may feel overwhelmed with guilt. Other times children are not allowed to own their painful feelings, causing them to stay stuck in Stage 2. For example, a child who is told that he should not be angry at his father for leaving may deny his feelings to himself but continue to seethe on the inside for years to come.

Parents can help their children move through Stage 2 at their own pace and emerge into Stage 3, a place of healing and growth. These children may still carry some sadness over their loss, but they have found a way to make sense of it and perhaps even partake some wisdom from the experience. The following tips can help you get through to your child under this challenging set of circumstances.

TIPS FOR HELPING A CHILD THROUGH THE STAGES OF GRIEF FOLLOWING A DIVORCE:

1. **Prepare your child for the divorce.** Children usually adjust faster and better if the parents have talked to them about the

divorce beforehand, rather than learning about the breakup as it happens traumatically when one parent storms out of the house leaving the other shocked and wounded. When possible, parents should approach their children together through a family meeting. Make sure you are not rushed and that you are both calm. Tell them in clear, straightforward language that they can understand. Being direct and clear will help communicate that you are serious about this, and that it is a decision that has already been made, one not open for reevaluation. Telling all your children together will give them some emotional comfort and support. Finally, be honest. Do not give them false hope or cushion the news with lies.

2. **Accept your child's feelings.** The rule of thumb is that all feelings are okay. It is only behavior that needs to be limited. For example, being angry with your parents for getting a divorce, even hating them, is to be understood and accepted. However, cursing your parents, breaking things, or other misbehaviors are not. These expressions are called "acting out," because the child is actually acting his feelings out through misbehavior. The parent's job is to help the child learn to express these feelings, even the ugly ones, through words rather than through misbehavior.

3. **Talk with your child about positive ways to cope.** Parents can help their children understand that people have various ways of coping with loss. Some of these ways are not good for them. For example, overeating, sleeping too much, using alcohol or other drugs, or doing other things that might make a person feel better in the short run, but cause new problems in the long run, are to be avoided. Instead, help the child or teen think about positive coping skills. For example, spending time with

friends, maintaining a normal schedule with school and activities, sharing your feelings, crying when necessary, and making
plans for the transition can all be helpful.

4. **Gently dispute irrational ideas and provide useful information
   and beliefs.** As you listen to your child's feelings and show
   acceptance, also tune in to what beliefs underlie his words. As
   we said, irrational beliefs can keep a kid stuck in grief for a
   long time. When you hear these mistaken ideas, it is important
   to gently but firmly correct them. In addition, there are ideas
   that you may not hear, but are typical of many kids going
   through a divorce. You will want to address these ideas, too,
   even if your child does not bring them up. We will cover some
   of these in the question section of this chapter.

5. **Involve your child in a plan of action.** We said earlier that
   action is the antidote for fear. Children of divorce are often
   filled with such fear. They may hide it behind their anger, but a
   child's vulnerability in the world almost always begs the question "What will happen to me now?" Talking with your child
   about plans for the future, according to his age level, reduces
   his fear by answering questions while showing him that he is
   not as powerless as he feels. Talk about his future involvement
   with the other parent. If you will be moving, bring the child
   into the discussion. No, children do not get a vote about
   whether to move or not, but even so, there are a lot of smaller
   decisions that can involve the child.

6. **See if your school or community has a special program for
   children of divorce.** Many schools now offer group programs
   for kids whose parents are divorced. These programs can help
   answer many of the questions that children have. In addition,

being in a group with other children going through a similar experience is often a tremendous help. Knowing you are not alone and helping each other cope can quicken the healing process.

7. **Use books or other resources to help you talk with your child.** There are many useful books written for kids of all ages about going through divorce. These books provide helpful information in their own right, but just as important, they provide a good starting place for a discussion with you. With young children, read the book together. Then talk about how the story is the same and different as to what you are experiencing. With older children and teens, you can let them read on their own and then discuss it together later. See what your child prefers, and be creative with your questions afterward.

QUESTIONS CHILDREN SOMETIMES ASK (AND POSSIBLE ANSWERS)

Young children, those under the age of five, will not usually understand the concept of divorce. They will simply know that one parent is no longer as involved in their lives as before. They may also pick up on any negative change in the custodial parent's mood and react to that. What young children need to know through this process is that they are safe, secure, and loved. You can communicate this message by taking time to play, cuddle, and read with them, maintaining a normal routine, encouraging them, and telling them that you love them.

As children get older, you will also need to address specific questions related to the divorce. If you have more than one child, it is best to talk with the children together. If possible, address them with your spouse to tell them about the upcoming divorce and to begin answering their questions. This helps let everyone know that you will both still be involved in their lives and that they are not losing a parent. You can later answer any individual questions as they come up. Some questions to be sure to cover:

Q. *What's going on here?*

Kids often know when trouble is in the air. They probably also know other kids whose parents have divorced and are probably wondering if your problems will end that way, too. In any case, once you have decided to divorce, you have to tell your children.

A. You probably know that your father (mother) and I have not been getting along too well for a long time. We have tried very hard to work out our differences, but we have decided that it just isn't going to get better between us. We have decided to get a divorce, and because this decision affects all of us, we wanted to talk to you about it and answer your questions.

Q. *Are you getting divorced because of me?*

This is the big question that haunts many kids whether they ever ask it or not. Either way, you want to sit them down, look them in the eyes, touch their arm or leg, and say with all sincerity something like the following. And you may need to say it several times over the next few months.

A. There is one thing that is very very important for you to know. This divorce is not your fault in any way, shape, or form. In fact, kids are never to blame for their parent's divorce, even kids who get into a lot of trouble and misbehave like crazy. A divorce is always the parents' choice. It happens when parents decide that they just cannot live together anymore. It is very sad, because it affects the kids as well as the adults. But the failure to get along is always the parents'. I am so sorry to be putting you through this, because I love you more than anything, and I don't want you ever blaming yourself for what's happened.

Q. *Why* are *you getting divorced?*

This question will usually have some anger behind it. Remember that except in cases of abuse or addiction, you are getting a divorce for your needs and not your child's. Most children would veto a divorce if given the power, so the least that you can do is give them a good reason. For example:

A. I want you to know that we have not taken this divorce lightly. We have worked very hard to solve our problems and still stay married, but we just have not been able to do it. Rather than continue fighting and being unhappy together, we have decided that we would be better off living separately. We also know that this isn't what you probably want, and for that we are both very sorry. We want you to be sure to understand that we still love you very much and we will continue to be your parents—nobody is divorcing you. You'll live with (Mommy), but you'll come stay with (Daddy) every other weekend and on some holidays and during a lot of the summer. . . .

Q. *What will happen to me?*

This is another huge issue with most children. There is a saying that no one is as concerned about losing an eye as the man with only one eye. When children have lost close contact with one parent, they are often overly concerned about losing the other. They may become clingy and even regress in behavior to a younger stage. They may wonder that if you can divorce their other parent, maybe you will divorce them, too. You will want to reassure them that you will be there for them and that they will be well taken care of. The specific of how you address this question will follow your own individual circumstances. Just keep in mind the need for empathy, reassurance, and good information. For example:

A. I know that this can be a scary time for children. You may be wondering what will happen to you and how things will be in the future. First thing you should know is that we are going to be just fine. Even though there will be changes, we are still going to have a good life together, and I'm going to make sure you are always taken care of. After all, I'm your mommy (or daddy) and that's my most important job—helping you grow up happy and healthy. We're going to be just fine together.

One of the things that will change is that we are moving to a new home. Now that we are a smaller family, we don't need as much room. I'm going to need your help in planning for this move. We have to decide how to pack, where to put things in the new house, and how to decorate. Can I count on your help?

Q. *What will happen to my relationship with Daddy (or Mommy)?*

Kids worry that once a parent has left that they will never see that parent again, or at least not often. Sadly, like in the opening vignette, this sometimes happens. Some parents do not have the mental health to stay involved after a divorce. Others lack the character and are just too plain self-centered. Most, fortunately, want to stay involved and make great efforts to keep the relationship alive and growing. These parents approach their role as parents with the respect and responsibility that it deserves. They need only find the words to communicate these important intentions to their children.

A. We both want you to know that you still have *two* parents who love you very much and want to spend time with you. We are going to make sure that we both get to spend lots of time with you. To begin with . . . (If you have not already told them when they will be staying with the other parent, this is a good time to do so.)

Q. *Do I have to choose sides in my loyalties?*

A wise child was once asked by her parents in the midst of a marital argument what she thought of the situation. Her sage answer was simply this: "It's none of my business." If all children and parents were so wise, there would be far fewer casualties of divorce. Marital and ex-marital arguments are none of the children's business, and children should be psychologically safe from having to choose sides. You can head off much turmoil in your children by letting them know this up front and by following through with your actions later.

A. There are a lot of things that your father (mother) and I don't always agree on. But one thing that we do agree on is that our problems are our problems and not yours. In other words, we don't want you to ever feel put in the middle between us. If one of us should forget this and ask you to take sides in an argument, or in any other way make you feel uncomfortable with our disagreements, here's what we'd like you to say: "It's none of my business." Or if you prefer, you can just say, "That makes me uncomfortable." That will remind us that grown-ups should handle their own problems and not dump them on their kids. What do you think?

Q. *Is it okay for me to be sad, angry, or hurt?*

Some kids think that courage means never having negative feelings, or at least not letting anyone else know that you do. Come to think of it, some parents think the same thing. The truth is that courage means persevering in spite of these negative emotions. Letting our kids know that it is okay to feel sad, angry, hurt, or anything else and helping them find appropriate ways to express these feelings can go a long way to helping them heal from the loss of divorce.

A. When families go through a divorce, there are usually a lot of strange feelings for everyone. Many of these feeling are painful, like sadness, hurt, fear, and anger. We all have them and it's perfectly okay to feel whatever you are feeling. What can help, though, is to share these feelings with somebody. If you want to tell me what you're feeling, I promise to listen and not criticize. I won't get mad at you for being angry with me, either. Maybe we can even find some creative ways for you to let some of these feeling out. Ever felt like hitting a punching bag?

Q. *Does this mean that you're going to dump all of your negative feelings on me?*

Kids are neither therapists nor parents and should not be expected to function as either. Neither are they our new best friends. Although it is okay for kids to see us sometimes sad, hurt, or angry, we don't want to turn them into our sounding boards, as we would be willing to do for them. To do so puts added stress on them to help make us feel better. Although some kids are emotionally strong enough to handle this added stress, the wise parent will limit sharing negative feelings at home, and instead find friends or a therapist who can offer adult support. Instead, what children need from parents is reassurance that the parent will eventually bounce back and not stay sad or angry forever.

A. I know that I've been pretty down lately and not much fun to be around. A divorce can really knock you for a loop. But the good news is that I won't be like this forever. I'm going through some grief right now, grief over the loss of our marriage. And when people grieve they often feel sad, hurt, or angry. But I'll move on after a while and will be a lot happier then. So don't worry, things will get better.

A Quick Review

Getting through to your kids during or after a divorce is a matter of planning and following through on a number of key messages. Helping your child understand and accept these beliefs can give them the courage and confidence to move through the stages of grief and emerge as a whole and healthy person. When possible, begin your talks before the divorce with both parents present. Then follow up with frequent talks in the days ahead. We also recommend using letters, E-mails, and other written communications to help make these messages get through. The idea is to reinforce your message in writing and to cover points that you may have missed during your talks. However, do not cop out and use a letter to break the news. This should always be done face to face, unless distance makes it impossible, and then a phone call should come before the letter. The following letter, written to a ten-year-old daughter, touches on some of the key messages you'll want to cover using language appropriate to your child's age.

Dear Shannon,

We are writing you together because we want you to know that even though we are getting a divorce, we are BOTH still very much your parents and that we both love you with all our hearts. Nothing can change that. You are our daughter and we will both continue to love you and take care of you. We told you that when we met to talk about the divorce, and we will probably tell you again a few hundred times, because we don't want you ever to forget it—even for a moment.

We have tried very hard to work out our problems without a divorce, but we just have not been able to do it. We know that this is very sad for us and for you, and we wish that things were different. Still, we have confidence that we will all come through this challenge okay, and that you will continue to grow into the healthy and happy person that you are becoming.

One thing that we want to be sure that you understand is that divorce is never the fault of the child. Even though kids sometimes think it is, it is always the fault of the parents. We want to be sure that you never blame yourself, even a little, for this divorce. In fact, you have every right to feel angry with us for letting you down. You might also find yourself feeling sad or even a little afraid. Whatever you feel is okay, and we hope that you will share some of those feelings with us. Letting them out can help. And we promise to listen and not criticize when you do share.

You might also see *us* feeling angry, sad, and even moody. This happens when people have lost something important to them, and it's called grief. Parents go through it just like kids do. We will try not to let our grief interfere with our normal lives. We will still go to work and take care of you. But if we do seem unhappy, we wanted you to know that this is normal and that it won't last forever. People heal from grief and can even be stronger and happier afterward.

As we said in our talk, there are also going to be some changes in our lives. Daddy will be living in an apartment, and you and Mommy will be moving to a smaller home. You will still get to be with Daddy every other weekend and on holidays, and he will still be just as much your father as he was before. You'll still live with Mommy, and she will take care of you day in and day out just like before. We both love you more than anything in the world, and we are going to make sure you are always taken care of.

Please ask either of us any questions that you have about what's going on or what's going to happen. We will try to include you as always in matters that affect you, and we want you to take an active part in making this change. You are a wonderful child and we are grateful to have you as our daughter.

We love you always,
Mommy and Daddy

Chapter 8

Driving . . .

the shortest distance between point A and point B is too often through the cemetery

The smashed metal mass that was once a car rested on the grass in front of the high school, a silent warning to all who passed. It was donated by the young man's parents in a valiant effort to make something useful out of something tragic. "How could this have possibly happened?" his mother wondered as she reflected over the events of the night that had changed her world so quickly. He had told her that he and his friend had planned to stay home because of an early day ahead. She had left them alone in the basement rec room as usual and gone to bed, her husband out of town. The phone call at 4:05 A.M. had jolted her awake with the impact of a siren. It was the police. They wanted to come over. When they arrived with a police chaplain, her worst fears became real in an instant. The tears flooded. Her mind raced to block the shock from overwhelming her. "Were they wearing seat belts?" she managed to stammer.

"No."

"Was there alcohol involved?"

"We think so."

Later she would confirm the missing six-pack of beer and wonder how he could have violated his promise of no drinking and driving. But right now she had to make the most difficult call of her life.

The phone in her husband's hotel room rang just before the alarm went off, waking him with the impact of a siren.

What Parents Need to Know

Don't you dare skip this chapter just because your child is only two and the only driving he's doing is driving you crazy! There is a reason we chose to begin with this topic. The reason is that a car will kill a child faster than anything else in the free world. Drugs, alcohol, tobacco, violence, and sex—they are all potentially deadly, but none of them comes close to killing as many young people as automobile crashes.

For fifteen- to twenty-year olds, auto accidents are the leading cause of death in the United States, accounting for about a third of the deaths of people in this age group. And from the moment your child has enough awareness to peer out over the restraint on his child safety seat and notice that he is being driven, he is learning how to drive—either safely or recklessly. There is no other activity in which children spend so much time watching adults perform a task as driving. By the time a child is sixteen and ready to get her driver's license, she has spent thousands of hours watching us drive. What we model for our kids by our attitudes and performance is indelibly imprinted in their minds. If we speed, drink and drive, become distracted, rage at other drivers, or engage in other unsafe practices while driving our children, we may as well begin hammering nails into their coffins. If we don't kill them ourselves, there is a good chance they will practice the same or worse unsafe practices and do it themselves later.

Sound too harsh? Maybe it is. But I just came from a town hall meeting about teen driving where parent after parent of teens who had died in automobile crashes talked through choked-back tears about their teens' tragic deaths. I have been to funerals where teens joyriding with other teens forgot about even the simple safety net of a seat belt and rolled their car into eternity. I have been to the home of a friend whose mother was killed by a drunken sixteen-year-old who crashed his car head-on into hers. And I watched, like the rest of the world watched, as Princes Diana was laid to rest, the victim of a high-speed car crash without a seat belt.

If car crashes were terrorist bombs, none of us would ever leave our homes. We would be too afraid of the frequency with which they occur to take the risk. But we have an awesome power to deny the risks that we accept each time we take to the roads. We deny and deny and deny, until one day we get that awful knock at the door, and a policeman is standing there, grim-faced, waiting to tell us the horrible news.

Five out of twenty teens will be involved in an auto accident, and one in twenty will be either fatally or seriously injured. About five thousand teenagers a year die in auto accidents. People sixteen to twenty are three times as likely to be involved in traffic deaths compared to the rest of the driving population. The risk is greatest the first year of driving, as sixteen-year-olds are twenty times more likely to have an accident than the general population. According to the National Highway Safety Administration, 32 percent of teen deaths involve speeding, 21 percent are due to drugs or alcohol, and 71 percent to not wearing seat belts. At least half of teen accidents are attributed to lack of experience. Finally, if you have a son, be especially worried. Teen boys are twice as likely as teen girls to die in a car crash.

We cannot think of a more important responsibility that we have as parents than to prepare our children to drive safely, and to begin while they are still young.

Show and Tell

When we discussed the importance of getting through to our kids' core values in chapter 3, we suggested that you "live, don't just give." Modeling safe driving yourself is fundamental. Even so, you can do more. Begin talking with your kids while they are still children about *why* you are doing certain things while driving. This will help them remember later when they are behind the wheel. For example:

ACTION: Putting on your seat belt first.
COMMENT: "I always put on my seat belt before I do anything else. That way it becomes a habit that I never forget."

ACTION: Asking, "Does everyone have on his seat belt?"
COMMENT: "Why do I always ask that?" Allow discussion, making sure that you point out that the driver is responsible for everyone else in the car.

ACTION: Saying: "Darn! I missed my exit," as you go down to the next exit and turn around.
COMMENT: "I'm amazed at how many people will cut across a lane of traffic to make an exit that they might miss. They risk their lives and the lives of others just to save five minutes. It's pretty crazy when you think about it."

ACTION: Driving slower at night, in the rain, or under other hazardous conditions.

COMMENT: "It's always smart to drive a little more slowly when it's wet outside. In fact, why is speed such a big part of many accidents?"

ACTION: Your kids are making a racket while you are driving, so you pull over to the side of the road.

COMMENT: "It is unsafe to drive with so much distraction. We will sit here until you can quiet down. And because this is my time you are wasting, you get to pay me for every minute we sit here at the rate of one dollar a minute." (This not only teaches the importance of not being distracted by passengers, a major cause of teen accidents, but also teaches the value of time and money.)

What Kids Need to Know

Talking about driving while you are driving is a great way to begin teaching your kids how to be safe drivers from an early age. However, once your kids begin to approach the magical age of sixteen, when they can get a learner's permit and get behind the wheel with an adult present, you want to make your instruction much more formal.

Do not be fooled into thinking that because a teen passes a licensing test at sixteen that he is a safe driver. Many states' licensing exams might be considered jokes if the consequences were not so serious. Some states require as little as the teen taking a paper-and-pencil test, driving around some orange cones in a parking lot, and parallel parking. This is a long way from finding yourself behind the wheel on a rainy night with oncoming headlights blinding you or trying to make a left-hand turn against three lanes of oncoming traffic during rush hour. Besides, we can't remember the last time that we heard of someone having a fatal accident while parallel parking.

Fortunately, many states are increasing the requirements for teen drivers and are going to graduated licensing programs. These programs place certain restrictions on sixteen- and seventeen-year-old drivers and often require more hours of behind-the-wheel instruction. However, the wise parent will still want to personally ensure that his or her teen is a safe driver before turning over the keys.

Learning a skill, whether playing basketball or learning to drive, requires hour after hour of practice. We suggest that your child have at least eighty hours of behind-the-wheel practice before getting a license. In addition, the following questions can help you begin to induce the right attitude and knowledge about driving. Remember to follow your question by listening *actively* and with *empathy*. We have also followed each question with a possible answer that you can share or discuss with your child. Further information can be found in the resource section at the end of this book.

Q. *Driving is one of the most dangerous things you will ever do, and the strange thing is that most people never even get that they are at risk. Why do you think driving is so risky?*

(It is difficult for adults, let alone teens, to imagine how incredibly powerful the impact caused by an auto crash can be on the human body. That is, unless you have experienced such an impact firsthand. Look for ways to make this message more relevant and real so that they will get just how dangerous this is.)

A. Have you ever heard the law of physics that a body in motion tends to remain in motion? When you are going 50 mph your body is also going 50 mph. If the car stops suddenly due to a crash, your body continues at 50 mph until it hits something that stops it, for example, a windshield, the steering wheel, or even an airbag. The speed of the impact can cause incredible damage, even death. Have you ever walked into a door that someone accidentally closed in your face? It hurt, didn't it? Well, you walk at about 3 mph. Imagine hitting a crushing mass of steel and glass at 50 mph or even 30 mph. What do you imagine that would feel like?

Q. *Do you think that beginning drivers are more at risk or less at risk than older drivers? Why?*

(The statistics are overwhelmingly clear that new drivers are much more likely to have an accident than more experienced drivers. Yet kids often do not get this basic fact. We want our kids to understand this so that they will drive more cautiously when they first get their license.)

A. It is amazing how fast things can seem to happen when you get into an auto wreck. Young drivers just don't have enough behind-the-wheel experience to know how to react when something goes wrong. It's not that they aren't careful, although that is sometimes true; it's just that they haven't had a chance to learn how to react. Let's take a look at some statistics that show what I mean. (Review the statistics from the beginning of the chapter with your teen. Share how important it is to be extra cautious during that first year of driving.)

Q. *What can we do to make sure that you become a safe driver?*

Brainstorm ideas. If she gives you the "I dunno," then maybe suggest that she do a little research. You might give her a few Web sites from the resource section of this book to get started or give her a book on the subject. For example:

A. For us to feel comfortable with you *ever* driving, we need a plan that will help ensure your safety. I want you to do some research and some thinking about it and then let me know your ideas. Let's talk about how we are going to use our driving practice time together. We've agreed that you will log 80 hours of behind-the-wheel time with a parent or driving instructor and keep a record of it in this book. Now, how should we use that time wisely? I mean, we aren't going to spend 80 hours driving around the mall on Sunday morning. (Be sure to come up with a list of activities that include practice in these areas: making turns, changing lanes, right-of-ways, backing up, driving in traffic, parking, passing, driving at night and in bad weather, parking on hills, and interstate driving.)

Q. *What do you think are the major factors that cause car accidents? Why does each increase the risk?*

If your teen doesn't know, again, you can give her some time to research the answer. Remember, the more effort she puts into finding the answer, the more she will own the information—the more she will get it. The answers include the following:

- Lack of driver experience. Without enough experience, drivers panic in some dangerous situations.

- Speed. Driving too fast makes it easier to lose control and harder to react to the unexpected. For example, if you come over a hill doing 30 mph and a child runs out toward the street, you have a good chance of stopping. If you were speeding through there, you would probably either hit the child or swerve off the road, injuring or killing yourself and your passengers. Second, when you impact something at higher speeds in an accident, the damage to the car and the riders is much greater.

■ Alcohol and other drugs. These impair judgment and reaction time. When under the influence, drivers often hit things they otherwise could avoid.

■ Fatigue. Recent research indicates that fatigue can be just as deadly on the road as DUI (driving under the influence). In addition to decreased reaction speed, all it takes is to fall asleep for a second, and you are off the road into a tree or an oncoming vehicle.

■ Horsing around with a carload of passengers. Teens especially are at much higher risk when driving other teens. The reason is simple: distraction. Someone in the backseat says something you can't quite hear and you turn around, "Say what?" and the next thing you know you are off the road. Because this is so difficult to guard against, many states are limiting the number of passengers that a sixteen-year-old driver can have in the car. If your state does not limit this, we suggest that you limit it to one passenger yourself.

Q. *During this year that you will be learning how to drive safely, I want you to pay particular attention to safety tips that we can come up with for different situations. For example: driving at school, around town, on the interstate, at night, in bad weather, in rural areas, and in general. What do you think would be a good way to keep track of all the good ideas that we come across this year?*

Try to get your teen to suggest keeping a list for each category in a driver logbook. This is a notebook that your teen can make to keep track of his 80 hours of practice in different situations. You can easily add a tips section to each category. In addition, collect articles from the newspaper about teen driving accidents, add them to the notebook, and discuss together.

Teen Driver Contract

We talked in chapter 2 about the power of commitments and especially the power of putting commitments into writing. A teen driver contract can help you clarify expectations and agreements, while reinforcing the commitment to drive accordingly. However, a common mistake that many parents and professionals make with contracts is to present them to the teen already written, just needing a signature. A contract is basically a deal between two or more people. And deals are usually negotiated though a give and take until all parties can agree. When parents attempt to dictate a deal to their teens they run the risk of hooking the teen's rebellious side. The teen may sign for fear of not getting to drive, but not only have they not bought into the parent's beliefs, they may actively undermine the contract whenever they get the chance. It may take longer, but it is much more persuasive to involve the teen in developing the contract. This does not mean that everything is up for negotiation. You should still stick to your limits about what you believe is safe. However, there is almost always room to negotiate some things *within* those limits. And when teens have a say in developing the rules, they are much more likely to feel that these are *our* rules and not *your* rules.

SAMPLE TEEN DRIVER CONTRACT

Understanding that the use of a motor vehicle is probably the most dangerous activity in which most people engage, and insomuch as the health and safety of our children and those they might injure are our primary concern and responsibility as parents, the following agreement is made between _____ (teen) _____ and _____ (parent or parents) _____ for the purpose of establishing guidelines for _____ (teen's) driving a motor vehicle. Due to the high stakes involved, any violation of these guidelines may result in the immediate loss of the driving privilege for an indefinite amount of time.

1. You will obey all driving laws and operate any vehicle you are driving in a safe manner.

2. You will only drive one passenger at a time, and we must first notify that passenger's parents that you are a first-year driver, before doing so.

3. Only you are allowed to drive a vehicle that we loan to you. You may not lend it to a friend or allow someone else to drive you.

4. If you are ever under the influence of alcohol or other drugs or in any other way unable to drive at full capacity, you are to call us for a ride home. This will not cause you to lose driving privileges.

5. You will not ride with anyone else who has been using alcohol or other drugs, is in any other way impaired, or who should not be driving. Instead, you are to call us for a ride home. This will not cause you to lose your driving privileges.

6. We will provide you with the use of a family car at no charge. You are to provide the cost of insurance, gas, and maintenance.

7. You will return home at agreed-upon curfews, according to the law in our state and our family agreements.

8. We will provide you and pay for a cell phone to be kept in your car. You are responsible for having it turned on and for answering it whenever we call.

There will probably be other items that you and your teen will want to discuss and add. The cell phone idea is something that more and more parents are using to help monitor teen behavior in general. As we go to press, more and more are also beginning to use satellite-tracking devices to know where the car is at any time. These systems are still relatively expensive, but when coupled with the Internet, they allow very accurate monitoring of your teen's whereabouts. Is it an infringement on your teen's privacy? Certainly. Is it worth the intrusion? That depends on the teen. For responsible teens who have a good track record for following the rules, it is probably not. For teens who test you at every turn, it might be the only way that you will feel comfortable with him driving.

QUESTIONS KIDS SOMETIMES ASK (AND POSSIBLE ANSWERS)

Q. *Will you buy me a car when I turn sixteen?*
Research from the National Highway Traffic Association indicates that teens who own their own cars have more accidents and lower grades than those who drive cars owned by their parents. We would therefore suggest that even if you choose to buy an extra car for your teen to drive that you keep it in your name.

A. I know you would love to have your own car at sixteen. Who wouldn't? But the fact is that cars are both expensive and dangerous. Here's what we are willing to do. We will buy a third car for you to drive. If you drive it safely and according to the contract that we signed (or will sign), then we will give it to you as a high school graduation present. (Of course, if an extra car is not in the family budget, then you have to tell your teen that and work out agreements for when she can borrow the family car or buy her own. In either case, your teen should be well aware that using the car is a privilege that is dependent on driving safely and responsibly.)

Q. *Why are you making such a big deal out of this? None of the other kids' parents are.*

A. Because we can't bear the thought of attending your funeral.

Q. *Aw, Mom, nothing bad is going to happen to me.*

A. It is *exactly* that attitude that worries me. And if you still have it when it's time to get your license, then you will be riding with me or in the big yellow cheese awhile longer.

Q. *What's a "big yellow cheese"?*

A. It a cool way of saying "school bus."

A Few Other Ideas

- Just prior to taking your teen for his license exam, set up an appointment with your auto insurance agent. Ask him or her to go over the information related to teen driving and how it impacts rates. Ask him to share what he has seen as a professional in the field and to encourage your teen to be especially careful. Often, our teens will listen to an adult outside the family more closely than she will to her own parents. In addition, an insurance agent has the added credibility of being a professional in the field.

- Chances are that your teen will be a passenger as well as a driver. Be sure to go over what you expect from him as a passenger. For example:

- You are only allowed to drive with drivers that we have approved of ahead of time. (Be very very careful of approving any sixteen-year-old driver. At a minimum make sure that he has had excellent driving instruction and is highly responsible.)

- If your driver has had any alcohol or other drug, then under no circumstances do you get in the car. You call us for a ride home, and you will be praised, not disciplined, for your good judgment.

- If you are riding with a group of kids and they are getting reckless in any way, then you ask to be let out at a safe place and you call us immediately. Again, there will be no negative consequences.

- Always wear your seat belt.

- If the driver is doing anything dangerous, ask him to stop. If he won't, ask to be let out and call us. If he refuses to let you out, tell him that your parents will have him hung by his thumbs.

- Here's a tip from personal experience. Two close relatives have been involved in relatively serious accidents because they trusted another driver's use of a turn signal. The other drivers each signaled for a left-hand turn. My relatives pulled out in front of the oncoming car to make a left-hand turn of their own. The other drivers did not make their signaled turn. Crash. Crash. Six cracked ribs to one and a totaled station wagon to the other. Who was at fault? In both cases it was my relative. I realize that this could be chalked up to bad genes in my family, but I'm willing to go out on a limb and suggest that many adults, as well as most teens, do not realize that a turn signal is no guarantee of a turn. The person traveling straight still has the right of way even if she signals for a turn and changes her mind. The prudent thing for the driver waiting to pull out and make a left is too make sure that the driver signaling to turn actually begins the turn before he pulls out in front of her. Please go over this with your teens until they get it.

A Brief Review

Driving is a privilege and not a right. We have a responsibility to our children, our fellow drivers, and pedestrians to ensure that our teens handle this privilege responsibly, or else not at all. Taking the time to get through about driving safety is maybe the most important job that modern society has created for parents in the last hundred years. The bloody deaths of five thousand teenagers a year bear cold witness to this fact. Start getting through when they are still young by modeling safe driving and talking to them about why you do the safe things you do while behind the wheel. When they become teens and get a learner's permit, use the time to talk about what is expected of them, provide at least 80 hours of driving practice, and consider signing a contract together specifying the rules for driving in your family.

Chapter 9

Friends . . .
people who need people

It is a perfect autumn Saturday when ten-year-old Carl approaches his friend Zack after their soccer game and asks him to spend the night. Zack angrily answers, "No, I'm busy." Carl walks away feeling that something is wrong, but has no idea what is bothering Zack or how to handle it. As luck or parenthood would have it, Carl's mother happens to overhear the exchange. She quietly observes the conversation, saying nothing. Later, she decides to call Zack's mother, a friend of hers, to see if something is bothering Zack. Zack's mother talks with her son and learns that he was hurt and angry with Carl for something that happened on the playground at school. It seems that when teams were chosen and Zack was selected for Carl's team, Zack heard Carl say, "Does he have to be on our team?" Carl's mother says that that doesn't sound like Carl, but she will check into it.

When she later talks to her son, Carl says that he didn't say anything when Zack was chosen. His mother realizes that not saying anything can be interpreted on playgrounds as a sign that you don't want the person on your team, and how that might hurt his friend's feelings. They talk about how to handle the situation and agree that Carl will apologize to Zack. A couple of days later at the next soccer game Carl approaches Zack and says, "I heard you thought that I said that I didn't want you on my team the other day. I'm sorry you thought that, because I do like having you on my team." Zack smiled broadly as his eyes lit up with pleasure. Problem solved.

What Parents Need to Know

The complexities of social relationships have fascinated and baffled sociologists, psychologists, anthropologists, apologists, and people of all kinds since humankind first discovered that alone we could never survive, but by forming small bands of cooperative people we could thrive. Even in our changing modern world, we continue to recognize the importance of getting along with others. As parents we want our children to cooperate, have friends and to be accepted. We hurt when they are rejected and take vicarious pleasure when they make good friends and enjoy the company of others. We worry about the influence of negative peer groups and notice ourselves checking out potential friends with an almost embarrassing scrutiny. We intuitively understand the influence and importance of others.

The psychological desire to belong is so well ingrained that the benefits of connecting with friends, family, and a loved one are still a core component of what it takes for most people to feel that they are thriving. When our people-to-people relationships falter, no amount of money or other survival stuff can bring us consolation. Women have traditionally known this fact of life better than men, and have sought to teach it to their children. In addition to getting through about the importance of relationships, parents of both sexes can also help teach their children the social skills that go into being a good friend and getting along with others.

When Peers Count More Than Parents

The downside of having friends is that sometimes the peer group becomes too important. Our long human history of wanting to fit in and belong creates a powerful desire to conform to any group that we have become attached to. Being left out, or worse yet, ostracized, is a very powerful motivator at all ages.

When children are young, parents usually exert a tremendous amount of influence on their lives. However, because the goal of childhood is to become independent of one's parents, a gradual shift from parental influence to peer influence begins as soon as the toddler goes off to his first child-care or play-group experience. When the relationship between parent and child is close, when there is plenty of parental nurturance, time to interact, stability in the home, respectful discipline and encouragement, the child continues to be primarily "adult oriented." This means she will look to parents and other adults for cues about how to behave and what values to adopt. However, when the parent-child bond is missing and a strong attachment has not formed, the child becomes "peer oriented." Such kids are more often antisocial, prone to misbehavior, and violent.

Even during adolescence when most people look to peer groups for increased acceptance, "adult oriented" kids will still be open to parental influence, whether through discipline, talking, or other means. But because the peer group will ultimately come to have greater and greater influence, it is helpful to teach our kids early how to pick good friends and to find creative ways to associate them with positive peers. Kids with strong parent-child relationships also tend to have higher self-esteem and greater confidence. This helps them pick out peer groups of similarly positive, motivated teens to befriend. These kids actually exert a positive influence over each other, using their influence to support each other in doing well academically, in sports, with relationship issues, and avoiding dangers such as smoking, drugs, and risky sexual activity.

Perhaps most interesting, adult-oriented children become the best friends and associates later on. These children have been treated respectfully by their parents, involved in problem solving and making choices, given a fair amount of freedom within the limits of the situation, loved, nurtured, played with, and taught how to give and take. They have both the emotional capacity for closeness that friendship requires and the skills to be a friend.

TIPS FOR HELPING CHILDREN DEVELOP GOOD PEER RELATIONSHIPS

1. **Use an authoritative style of parenting.** Researchers such as Diana Baumrind have found that this style of parenting is characterized by a lot of nurturance and a modest amount of discipline. Nurturing includes such things as affectionate and friendly interactions; playing together; consideration of the child's feelings, desires, and needs; interest and involvement in his activities; respect for her point of view; pride in her accomplishments; support for her problems; and expressions of love. Discipline in the authoritative style is characterized by fair rules that are explained to the child; the use of encouragement and other positive reinforcers; problem solving; and the use of consequences in which children are expected to make up for their misbehavior. The authoritative style is contrasted with an autocratic style, in which discipline is too harsh and nurtu-

rance is too little, and the permissive style, in which nurturance is apparent, but discipline is lacking. The research suggests that children raised in authoritative homes are more socially competent, well-liked by their peers, and yet less likely to be negatively influenced by their peers.

2. **Teach social skills.** There are thousands of teachable moments scattered throughout the life of a child when a parent has the opportunity to get through about how to be a friend or just plain get along with others. From the basics of shaking hands and looking the person in the eyes when you greet someone and taking turns on the playground, to more complicated skills such as empathizing with another person's feelings, point of view, and solving problems cooperatively, parents can help their children learn how to handle relationships with people effectively. This is done in a number of ways, for example: talking with kids routinely about what's appropriate in different situations; talking about good manners and encouraging your kids when they practice those same good manners in public; mediating childhood disputes in ways that teach such values as fairness, taking turns, sharing, and consideration of others; and heart-to-heart talks with your child when problems with peers emerge, as they inevitably will for all children.

The mother in the opening vignette went to unusual lengths to help her child learn a lesson from his playground experience. First, she didn't fall into the pitfall of lecturing her son: "Carl! That is no way to treat a friend. Now you pick up the phone this instant, call Zack and apologize!" That would have just created hurt and resentment on Carl's part, damaged their own relationship, and probably not helped the situation with Zack, either. She also avoided the opposite trap of springing to her son's defense and telling the other mother: "I'm sure Zack must have heard wrong. Carl would never say something like that." Instead she recognized that kids do sometimes say things out of character and that she could take a nonjudgmental stance and quietly investigate. Finally, she avoided doing nothing. Although the boys would probably have gotten over it soon enough on their own, this was a teachable moment for getting through to her son about social situations. For example, Carl probably learned that at times saying nothing can be interpreted as a sign of disrespect and disloyalty, and that it is important to stand up for your friends verbally. He also learned something about mending bridges by clarifying misunderstandings and apologizing for one's own part in creating them.

3. **Be nonjudgmental and gentle.** If your child feels attacked when you talk about ways she could have better handled a situation, she will probably become defensive. Defensiveness has the effect of closing the mind to possible change. Instead, the child looks for ways to blame others or justifies his own behavior, making it very difficult to get through. On the other hand, a gentle, empathetic posture can help your child know that you are on his side. ("I know you were disappointed when Zack sounded like that. What do you suppose was going on with him?" This has the effect of reducing resistance and opening the mind to possible changes.)

4. **Allow children to decide how to handle their own problems.** When children and teens have problems with peers, this is not a time for discipline or control. The parent's better role is that of an experienced consultant who wants the best outcome for her client. Letting your child know that you are not trying to

take over and that the final decision is hers reduces defensiveness and lets you ultimately have more influence in her decisions.

5. **Do not get angry if your child chooses to handle a problem differently than you would.** Of course, it is hypocritical to say that the decision is your child's, but then to respond with anger if she makes a decision with which you disagree. Show your child the respect of letting her try out her own decisions, knowing that if they do not work out, you have another learning opportunity to discuss.

6. **Never say, "I told you so."** Nothing ruins a good lesson like a gloating parent. The world is filled with people of all ages who continue to make bad choices partly because they do not want their parents, deceased or alive, to continue to hold it above their heads that they knew best. At least by making bad choices, they unconsciously reason, they can deprive their parents of gloatingly taking the credit. Conversely, parents who give all the credit to their children for good choices have children who continue to listen to them, consider their opinions, and then act according to their best judgment of all the information.

What Children Need to Know

The secret to getting along with people from mere acquaintances to a lifelong romantic partner is essentially "The Golden Rule." No wonder that it is the cornerstone of so many of the world's great religions. When we "do unto others as you would have others do unto you," and "do not do to your neighbor that which you do not want your neighbor to do to you," we get along remarkably well with others.

The reason that this concept is so powerful is that it is a lot easier to know what *we* would like and how *we* would feel than it is to know what others like and feel. But the beauty is that we are all more alike than different, so that if kids will treat other kids like they want to be treated, they will usually hit the mark. It then becomes a short trip from the Golden Rule to teaching children empathy for others. Empathy essentially means putting oneself in the other's shoes and really feeling what the other person is feeling. When a person can do this, that person becomes ready for true friendship. Before then, we are just playmates at any age. The following sorts of questions can help you teach your child to understand feelings better and to see things from another person's perspective.

1. Zack sounded angry to have responded that way. What do you think he was angry about?

2. How do you think that you would have felt if someone had said that about you?

3. What do you think she was thinking when she did that?

4. How do you think she felt?

5. It sounds as if she was *embarrassed* . . . (or whatever emotion you think is accurate).

6. It sounds as if you were feeling . . .

7. If it had been you in that situation, what would you have wanted the other person to do?

Coach Your Kids About How to Avoid Peer Pressure

We are all more or less susceptible to peer pressure. If our friends are talking about how good a movie is, chances are we will want to go see it. If we are sitting in a theater after a performance that we thought was okay, but not great, and everyone else rises to give a standing ovation, chances are that we stand up, too. If we are over at some friend's home and they offer us some cocaine, that's presumably where we draw the line and say, "Are you crazy?"

The reason that we are so susceptible to peer pressure is twofold: 1) It saves us time. In today's busy world we do not have time to check out everything for ourselves, so we rely on the judgment of peers about many matters as a shortcut. 2) We want to be accepted.

Most people do not want to stand out as the sore thumb, so we stand up in the theater and applaud whether we really want to or not. After all, what's the harm? And here is where a major distinction comes in to play. Healthy functioning people with reasonably good self-esteem know to say no when giving in to peer pressure has a high risk of negative consequences. They also learn *how* to say no in ways that do not leave them feeling foolish or alienating otherwise good friends. Teaching our kids this tactful art will bolster both their willingness and ability to reject dangerous peer pressure when it arises. Young children can simply be taught to say "no" or "I don't want to" when asked to do something that they know is wrong. However, with older children and teens, saving face becomes a bigger issue. When peers put subtle or direct pressure on these kids to do something that they know is either wrong or too dangerous, the following steps can help them sidestep the pressure while still saving face:

1. **Ask clarifying questions.** If something sounds suspicious, teach your kids to ask the kinds of questions that will illuminate the

hidden risks. For example, if someone asks your ten-year-old to watch a video over at his house, these kinds of questions can be helpful: What video do you want to watch? What's it rated? Who else will be there? Will your parents be home? If your child finds out that the video is rated R and that a big brother who lets them watch anything they want is in charge, and he knows that he is not allowed to watch R-rated videos, then it's time to say no gracefully.

2. **Tell them the problem.** At this point it is helpful for your child to tell the other kid or kids the problem he has with going along. For example, he might say, "I have a problem with that because my parents don't allow me to watch R-rated videos." (Other examples might include: ". . . because it's illegal to drink under 21"; ". . . because drugs are addictive and can kill you, or at least get you into all kinds of trouble"; ". . . because I don't think it's right to treat her that way. I mean how would you like it if somebody did that to you?"

3. **Suggest an alternative.** Sometimes kids can take the leadership role by suggesting an acceptable alternative to the group. This helps avoid the problem for everyone, plus lets your child continue to be with his friends. For example, "It's too nice a day to watch a movie anyway. Why don't we go skating instead?" If that doesn't work and the group insists on doing what they were planning to do, then it's time to move on.

4. **Move on.** At this point you hope that you have instilled in your child the courage to start walking. Maybe he will also recall you telling him, "Remember, son, character is having the courage to do the right thing even when you could get away with doing the wrong thing." If he knows this and values his

character more than the temporary acceptance and company of his peers, he will start walking while saying something like "Well, I guess I'll have to pass, but if you change your mind I'll be skating over at my house."

Take the time to go over these steps with your older children and teens and then role-play some situations together that might come up. The more practice they get saying no to peer pressure with you, the easier it will be to say no under pressure from their peers.

Questions Kids Sometimes Ask (and Possible Answers)

Young Children

Young children will generally just state a problem rather than asking a question. For the sake of example, we will state the problem and put the implied question in parentheses.

Q. *David hit me! (What are you going to do about it?)*

When young children hit, there is a tendency for adults to want to investigate, find out who the guilty party is, then sentence that party to a punishment. This is a trap. It is very difficult to determine how conflicts with young children get started, and seeking to punish one party often leads to a round of "But he hit me back first." Instead, it is better to take a mediation role in helping kids learn to solve their problems peacefully. Then, let them know that there is a "no hitting" rule and that if there is any more hitting by anyone, then you will separate them both for a period.

A. You sound angry. Did it hurt? . . . I'll tell you what . . . let's talk to David and see if we can figure out what happened and how you guys can play together without hitting.

Q. *Kali is mean to me! (How do I make her be nice?)*

Since no young child is nice all the time, chances are that this is just one of the ups and downs of learning how to get along, as they also try to get what they want. True, Kali may also be bratty, moody, and spoiled, but it is better to use the opportunity as a teachable moment than an indictment of a young child. If Kali is there, then again, mediate to find out what the conflict is about and how you can teach them to handle it by sharing, taking turns or some other skill. If the other child is not there, you might say something like this:

A. It sounds as if she hurt your feelings. Want to tell me what happened? (Then afterward . . .) What do you think you could do next time you are together to make it better? (Help brainstorm some ways that she could work it out the next time such a conflict happens. For example, if Kali called her a "baby," you might suggest: "Well, one thing you could tell her is that you don't like to be called names and that if she wants to play with you, then she has to stop doing that.")

OLDER CHILDREN AND TEENS

Q. *Why wasn't I invited to the party?*

Any child who makes it all the way through school without ever being left out is far too popular. As always, begin by responding to your child's feelings in an empathic way to let her know that you care about how she feels and are on her side. Then help her explore what may be going on in her world. Finally, there may be some actions that she can take either to be included next time or to find her own group of friends.

A. I'm sorry, honey. I know that can be disappointing. Nobody likes to be left out, even though it happens to all of us sometimes.

What do you think happened? (You can explore this by asking questions such as: Did she invite everyone else or were other kids not invited? How well did you know the girl giving the party? Have you ever invited her to anything? What can you do to become better friends with her or some of the other kids in that group? Or would you be better off with another group of friends? If you happen to uncover a problem with your child that causes her to be left out, then you'll want to address it sensitively. The following question suggests some ways of doing this.)

Q. *Why don't the other kids like me?*
There are a number of answers to this question, but they all start with the same beginning. . . .

A. Hmm, I know how bad that must feel. But tell me something: How do you know that no one likes you? (If your child is just feeling slighted about not being invited to a party in which a number of other kids were not invited, either, then you may want to help her get things into perspective.) I know it feels bad not to be invited, but I want you to know that nobody always gets invited to everything. That certainly doesn't mean that nobody likes you. It may mean that somebody doesn't like you enough to invite you to her party, or maybe she just doesn't know you as well as she does some of the others. (However, if your child is right and the other girl really doesn't like her, then you can either explore the problem seeing how your child might improve the relationship, or you might take this tact): Honey, I guess you should know that not everybody you meet is going to like you. People who think they have to be liked by everyone are either disappointed a lot or else they try so hard to please everyone else that they rarely feel pleased themselves. (Finally, if you suspect or uncover a major social problem and your child really is disliked by most kids, then you want to address this with your child, the school counselor, and if necessary, a child or adolescent therapist. Be honest, but say it in a way that gives hope that things will improve. For example: Okay, let me see if I have it straight. Right now you don't have a lot of friends. In fact it sounds like there are a lot of kids who don't like you very much. That doesn't feel good and you want to change it. Is that the situation? Then let's see what we can do to change that. First, do you have any ideas about what is bothering them about you? If neither of you know, then call your child's teacher and enlist her help. She will know. Then together you can work on a plan for developing better social skills and correcting problems. Also, be aware of any extra stress that your child is under. For example, are there marital problems, a chronic illness, or a difficult divorce? Did someone close to your child die recently? If something is distressing your child then you will need to address that problem or bring in some professional counseling help. Also be aware of your child gravitating toward a negative social group. Kids who feel left out and inferior often band together for comfort. Unfortunately, they are often negative influences on each other encouraging antisocial behavior, disrespect for school, and involvement with tobacco, alcohol, and drugs. Again, get some outside help and look for positive peer groups with which to get them associated. For example, a religious youth group, a sports team, choir, or other outside interest can offer opportunities to make positive friends while strengthening self-esteem.

Q. *How do I say no if I don't want to go out with someone without hurting his feelings?*

Being sensitive to the feelings of others is a quality that you want to encourage, but so is honesty. Teaching kids to make up social lies to avoid hurting someone is considered acceptable in much of our society; however, like all dishonesty, it can create more problems down the road for everyone. Instead, you might talk to your child about the difference between a "hard no" and a "soft no." A hard no comes across as brutally honesty and can hurt a lot. It is usually accompanied by a cold tone of voice with little concern for the other's feelings. A soft no is still a rejection, but a statement of empathy or appreciation accompanies it. For example:

A. That's a tough one. I'm glad to see that you care about the other person's feelings, though. That's important. Sometimes it's worth going out with someone one time to see if you have more in common than you thought. If there is, then you can see where the relationship leads. If not, and he asks you out again, you have the same problem about how to say no without hurting his feelings. First, I think that you ought to know that you can't be responsible for other people's feelings. You can just be responsible for how you treat them. Most people want to be treated honestly and kindly. They don't want you to lie to them and make up excuse after excuse every time they call. Yet they don't want you to be cold and tell them that you just aren't interested, either. What I found that worked for me was to say something like this: "I really appreciate you asking me. That's very sweet of you. But right now I'd rather us just stay friends and not start dating. But thanks so much for asking me. That was really nice. I'll see you in school tomorrow, okay?" I know it will still hurt their feelings a little, but I always made a point to look for them in school the next day and say hello. That way they knew that I wasn't rejecting them as a person. What do you think would work for you?

Q. *How do you get to be popular?*

A. I'm not sure I know the answer to that one, honey, because I always considered being popular to be overrated. In fact, the world is filled with people who were popular in school and then miserable afterward. I think the key is really about how to a good friend. I found that getting along with most everybody was important; having a few friends that you liked to do things with was good, too; and having a best friend that you could really share your deepest secrets with was the best of all. What are some of the qualities that you look for in people you want to be friends with? (This is a great opportunity to talk about such values as honesty, fun, hard work, encouragement, loyalty, and others. Then discuss which of these values your own child exemplifies and which she can work to improve.)

A Brief Review

Learning how to get along with others is a key component of life in any society. You can strengthen your child's social skills and values while getting through about such issues as peer pressure, how to be a friend, how to care about other people's feelings, and how to solve problems peacefully. Finally, teaching children empathy for others and helping them learn to apply the Golden Rule will give them a foundation for not just getting along with others, but for being a genuine friend and partner.

Chapter 10

Illness and Disability . . .

It's not what you have, but what you do
with what you have.

When Helen was a young child her parents discovered that she could not see, hear, or speak. Because she was so severely limited in her ability to receive information and to communicate her needs, her parents also mistakenly believed that she was mentally retarded as well. She wasn't. In fact, she was an exceptionally bright child, but this was impossible to know at the time.

Being loving and compassionate people, not to mention reasonably well off, her parents made sure that she was well-cared for and had all of her physical needs met. Over time Helen learned that she could have food by stomping her feet and making anguished guttural sounds whenever she liked. During mealtimes she was allowed to wander around the table while the family ate, taking food from anyone's plate whenever she wanted and shoveling it into her mouth with both hands, creating whatever mess was to be made. Her mother or a nurse would wash her, dress her, and do whatever else she needed. Her frequent temper tantrums were accepted as part of her struggle and handicap.

It wasn't until they hired a special tutor by the name of Anne that things began to change. First, Anne explained to the parents that their indulgence and low expectations of their daughter was a greater handicap than her physical limitations. She insisted that they allow her to provide the discipline that Helen desperately needed in order to learn. Through patient teaching and a refusal to allow the very spoiled little girl's tantrums to get her what she wanted, Anne was able to break through the barrier that had separated Helen from humanity. She began to learn polite manners, how to care for herself, and then in one dramatic moment, the concept of language when she signed the word *water* as the cool, clear liquid poured over her hand.

The true story of Helen Keller and Anne Sullivan (*The Miracle Worker*) has inspired millions as it poignantly illustrates the power of perceived limitations to hold back the human spirit and the equal power of courage and perseverance to overcome real handicaps and allow the spirit to soar. For the millions of children and parents who are challenged with disabilities and handicaps of all kinds, it is a story of triumph and hope.

What Parents Need to Know

The term *disability* refers to people who have physical, intellectual, emotional, or social impairment that substantially limits one or more major life activities. These include such problems as attention deficit/ hyperactivity disorder (ADHD), autism, cerebral palsy, deafness and hearing loss, Down's syndrome, emotional disturbance, epilepsy, learning disabilities, mental retardation, severe and/or multiple disabilities, speech and language impairments, spina bifida, traumatic brain injury, and visual impairments. With approximately 5.5 million children (about 10 percent of the public school population) receiving Special Education services, it is clear that the challenges of dealing with disability affects a great many families as well as our entire society as a whole. When you add to this the thousands of children and parents who also cope with chronic illnesses such as asthma, diabetes, leukemia, aplastic anemia, AIDS, allergies, Alzheimer's, cancer, chronic fatigue syndrome, cystic fibrosis, depression, epilepsy, lupus, Lyme disease, migraines, multiple sclerosis, Parkinson's disease, and many other conditions, then the magnitude of the challenge of helping these children develop their full potential for the benefit of themselves and their communities is tremendously important to us all.

Know Your Disability or Illness

There is nothing more motivating in education than relevancy, and there is probably nothing more relevant to a parent than a disability or chronic illness in the family. Whether it is a parent, child, or other family member that is directly affected, face the problem directly and use your best educational efforts to learn all you can. Your knowledge can be a powerful ally in helping a child cope with the challenges of her disability or illness, or to cope with another's. Medical and educational specialists are your first line of information. They can tell you the facts and provide reading material to help you understand the particular challenges, treatments, and coping strategies for helping your family adapt to changing needs.

A second powerful ally can be found in the support of people who have experienced similar challenges. Support groups for almost every conceivable problem now exist in communities throughout the nation. These groups provide the encouragement to keep going when frustration begins to get you down and the practical wisdom of people who have been there, done that, and learned what works from what doesn't. We cannot begin to duplicate such knowledge in a single chapter, and even if we could, it would never mean as much coming from us as from someone who has walked the same path as you. To find groups in your own area check the local newspaper for listings; check with a religious organization; ask your child's school or pediatrician; or consult with a helping professional such as a counselor or therapist. If you live in a small community and a support group for your child's disability is not available, then you are living in the right moment in history. The Internet has made it possible to join a chat group or forum with people from all over the world who share similar problems and concerns. Check our resource chapter for Web sites or just go to a search engine and type in the name of your child's disability and the words *support group*. For example: *ADD* and *support groups*. You will come up with a list of possible groups to explore.

Finally, you will want to find books, articles, videos, and other resource materials to help you better understand the disability or illness and ways to deal with it effectively. Your local library, a good bookstore, and the Internet are all good places to start your search.

Know Your Rights

During the past thirty years there have been some very significant pieces of legislation in the area of disability. The Americans with Disabilities Act passed in 1992, making it illegal to discriminate against someone with a physical or mental disability based on that disability. This applies to job opportunities, as well as requiring that public accommodations must make reasonable modifications in order to accommodate persons with disabilities. For example, making rest rooms wide enough to accommodate a wheelchair or modifying equipment in a child-care setting so that a child who cannot walk is able to pull himself up would be considered "reasonable."

The Individuals with Disabilities Education Act (IDEA) was first passed in 1975 and then amended in 1997. The main purposes of this act as stated in the law are:

(1) (A) to ensure that all children with disabilities have available to them a free appropriate public education that emphasizes special education and related services designed to meet their unique needs and prepare them for employment and independent living;

(B) to ensure that the rights of children with disabilities and parents of such children are protected; and

(C) to assist States, localities, educational service agencies, and Federal agencies to provide for the education of all children with disabilities;

(2) to assist States in the implementation of a statewide, comprehensive, coordinated, multidisciplinary, interagency system of early intervention services for infants and toddlers with disabilities and their families;

There are other laws in place that also support the right of children with disabilities to be effectively educated. The bottom line, however, is that millions of children who were once deprived of appropriate education are now thriving in schools throughout the land. The role of parents is to make sure that their children are receiving this opportunity and to work with the special education teachers and other professionals in their school system to support their work.

Know Your Child's Teachers and Other Professionals

There are many professionals who will be excellent resources for you and your family. Educators, doctors, psychologists, social workers, tutors, and others who are experts in various disabilities can help your child develop to her full potential. However, you know your child best, and your knowledge can be a huge resource to them as well. Perhaps even more important are your roles as an advocate for your child and a cheerleader for everybody. This is a delicate balance. As an advocate, you want to ask questions and make sure that your child is getting the best treatment, education, or help possible. At times this may require you to become assertive, even confrontational. At the same time, you also want to encourage the people who are working with your child and let them know how much you and your family appreciate all that they are doing. Encouragement brings out the best in people, even professionals. When your role calls for assertiveness, be sure that you confront respectfully and then look for opportunities to encourage. The positive relationship that you build with these people is important to them and to your family.

Help Your Child Build Courage

The primary risk inherent in any disability or chronic illness is the threat to the child's development caused by the problem itself. However, a secondary, and in many ways more insidious, risk is the damage that a disability or chronic illness can do to a child's courage, self-esteem, and confidence. The damage that is often done by well-meaning parents and others in this regard can be more harmful than the original problem itself. Remember how Helen Keller's

150

well-meaning parents turned her into a spoiled tyrant without self-discipline or the ability to care for herself in the slightest? Their over-protection and pity robbed young Helen of the opportunity to develop her strengths. The following tips can help you avoid this mistake while building your child's courage to meet life's challenges.

TIPS FOR HELPING A CHILD BUILD COURAGE AND SELF-ESTEEM

1. **Build on strengths.** Will Rogers once said that we are all ignorant, just on different subjects. Likewise, we all have our weaknesses, just in different areas. Children with disabilities and illness have weaknesses that are more obvious and sometimes more pronounced. However, all children also have strengths. Building on strengths can either overcome weaknesses or at least compensate for them. Visually impaired children can become attuned to sounds and smells when crossing a street. A young adult with MS who was limited to a wheelchair once used his mind to develop an expertise in astrophysics and helped millions of people better understand the universe. A restless child who would probably now be diagnosed as having ADHD once channeled his restlessness into inventiveness and gave us the electric lightbulb and phonograph. The contributions of these individuals, Stephen Hawking and Thomas Edison, respectively, bear testimony to the importance of building on strengths.

   Progress, however, is often slow, proceeding in small steps and requiring courage and persistence. Anne Sullivan first taught Helen Keller how to behave like a civilized human being. She encouraged Helen with every step of progress along the way. She built on these baby steps to teach her to dress and wash herself, again offering more praise and encouragement.

151

As Helen's courage grew, she took more risks and eventually learned to understand language and communicate through sign language. The courage that had first been given from without through her teacher now came from her successes as she mastered one new skill after another on her way to becoming a national figure of her time.

2. **Avoid pity.** Your child's courage cannot grow in a garden watered by pity. Feeling sorry for a disabled person sends the wrong message. It says in effect, "You are pitiful." And once a person accepts herself as pitiful, then there is very little motivation left to build on strengths and actualize her potential. Instead, help your child to face her problems courageously as obstacles to be overcome, not as barriers from which to turn back. By all means, be loving and compassionate, firm at times and gentle at others, but work past the normal feeling that life has somehow been unfair to you. You have been given a problem to solve, and in the solution to that problem you may discover, as many others have discovered, that there is also a rare gift.

3. **Avoid overprotection.** A simple rule of thumb for all parents is to never do for a child on a regular basis what the child can do for himself. Favors are okay, but to regularly tie a child's shoes rather than teaching her to tie her own shoes or insisting that she do it for herself is overprotection. And overprotection robs children of the courage and self-esteem that comes from struggling and succeeding. Parents of children with disabilities and chronic illness are particularly susceptible to this risk. For one thing, their children often truly require them to do things that they cannot do for themselves. In addition, in a misguided

attempt to make life easier, these parents sometimes do too much for their children and deprive them of the right to strengthen their wings in the struggle. Help teach your child to cope with life to the best of her ability by putting forth the effort to do her best.

4. **Encourage risk taking and growth.** The opposite of overprotection is to actively encourage your child to risk failure and to take the next step. Have positive expectations and help him learn to set realistic goals. Then break these goals down into baby steps, and take them one step at a time. Encourage the effort and perseverance whether successful or not. Make sure that your child owns her successes and recognizes that setbacks are part of growth. Movement toward her goals will help build the self-esteem and courage to set other goals and continue to try.

5. **Show acceptance and love.** Although courage and self-esteem can be generated by a child's successes, the deepest form of these important qualities comes from believing that just as you are, you are already good enough. Your acceptance of your child as a wonderful part of your life, disabilities and all, sets the foundation for such a belief. To get through at this level requires a genuine appreciation for this person with whom you have been blessed. Tap into that primal instinct to love and protect your child, and then communicate in words such as: "I'm really glad that you are my son (or daughter)"; "You are such a special part of my life and I love you so much"; "You are such a joy to be with; How did I get so lucky?!" Say it also through your actions when you take time to kiss, hug, cuddle, and play together.

QUESTIONS KIDS SOMETIMES ASK (AND POSSIBLE ANSWERS)

Q. *Why is my brother so . . . different?*

It is important for siblings to be informed about the disability or chronic illness for both children's sake. Take the time to help them understand the nature of the problem as well as the role that they can play in helping keep siblings active and involved. Research also shows that children who have a sibling with a disability tend to become more empathic and altruistic, have a higher tolerance for differences, and possess an increased sense of maturity and responsibility. As always, talk with your child honestly and at a level appropriate for his age. Give enough details to explain the situation, but then take your cues from him. Older kids may ask more questions and can be actively involved in researching the disability and making plans to help.

A. In most ways, your brother is pretty much like other kids. But he also has a certain type of condition called _____. This makes it harder for him to do certain things like _____ and _____. He didn't do anything to cause this, it just happens sometimes, and nobody really knows why. In some families when something like this happens, people start feeling sorry for themselves or even blame the person. Do you think that's fair?

A. (Cont.) Your brother needs our support. Sometimes he may need us to do things for him that other kids can do for themselves. We also need to teach him to do things for himself that may be difficult at first. But he is lucky. Do you know why? Because he has a family that loves him and cares about him and who will take the time to help him. That includes you, too. He is really lucky to have you for a sister (brother). Do you want to talk about some ways that you can help?

A. (Cont.) We will probably spend more time with your brother helping him deal with his disability than we would if he didn't have this problem. Sometimes it may seem to you that we are spending too much time with him and ignoring you. You may be a little angry with that. That's okay. Just tell us if that happens, and we'll try to make sure that we spend more time with you, too. Will you let us know?

Q. *Why is Mommy sick all the time?*

When a parent has a disability or a chronic illness children need to be told what is wrong, how it will affect the family and what is likely to happen in the future. You can help reduce your child's anxiety by getting him to do something active to help.

A. (**Young children**) I can tell you are worried about Mommy. She hasn't been herself lately, because she has something called _____, and it makes her unable to do things sometimes. There will be times when she has to stay in bed and can't do very much. Other times she will be able to play with you and do other things that she loves to do. In our family when someone is sick we all pitch in and help. Would you like to help by making Mommy a get-well card?

A. (**Older children and teens**) You sound _____ (worried, concerned, frustrated, or whatever feeling you perceive). Would you like to know what is going on? (If he says yes . . .) Mommy has a problem called _____. What this means is that _____. The doctors have told us that the best thing to do for her is _____. We have always pitched in and helped whenever someone has been sick in our family, and this time Mommy really needs our help. We don't know exactly what will happen in the future, but we do know that it can help if we all show her our support by letting her know how much we love her and that we want to help her handle this challenge. How do you feel about what I've just told you? (Encourage your child to talk about his feelings, letting him know that whatever he is feeling is okay—even if he is angry or embarrassed.) Would you like to talk about some things that you could do to help? (Brainstorm together— from helping out around the house or with siblings to doing research about the illness or disability on the Internet. Then look for opportunities to encourage your child's positive actions in the days ahead and continue talking regularly.)

Q. *Why am I dumb?*

About 5 percent of children in public education have a learning disability. This is a neurological disorder that interferes with their ability to process information in one or more areas such as reading, writing, and spelling (dyslexia); math (dyscalculia); or motor skills (dyspraxia). Because of these problems such kids often feel "dumb" in spite of the fact that they are usually average or above average in intelligence and often excel in other areas of functioning. Additionally, learning disabilities often occur with attention deficit (hyperactivity) disorder (ADD/ADHD), which can involve hyperactivity, distractibility, and impulsivity, making it even more difficult for the child to learn. Because your child may ask this question before you know that she has a learning disability, your first response should acknowledge his feelings of frustration and enlist his cooperation about getting tested to see what the problem is all about.

A. School can be very frustrating, can't it? I bet some days you wish you never had to go to school again. All kids feel like that sometimes. You seem to be feeling that way a lot lately, though, and I know that your grades haven't been what you'd like them to be. I'm not sure what the problem is, but I know one thing for sure, you certainly aren't dumb. I've seen how quick your mind can work, and you have plenty of intelligence. But I do think that we need to find out why you are struggling. I think it may be time to talk to your teacher. Then we can figure out how to help you better. What about if I give her a call? Once you talk to your child's teacher, you will probably want to schedule an evaluation through the school psychologist or an independent psychologist. Let's assume the results show that your child does have a learning disability. The psychologist can explain it to you and your child. Afterward, however, talk with your child again about the problem, letting her know the positive side as well as the challenging side of LD. Then together with your school's Special Education Department, plan an appropriate course of action that includes not only the school, but also you and your child.

A. I want to talk with you about the meeting with the school psychologist. What did you get from that meeting? (This will give you a chance to correct any misunderstandings, before moving on.) Well, one thing that I felt during that meeting was relieved. What I mean by that is that it's good to know what the problem is so that we can attack it head on. Lots of kids have learning disabilities, and like the psychologist said, they can learn to compensate and do very well in school anyway. In fact, I know that some really successful people throughout history have had learning disabilities or ADD, for example, Thomas Edison and lots of successful business people. In fact some people think that people with LD or ADD have some special gifts as well as their limitations. The ones that do well learn to develop their gifts and compensate for their weaknesses. In any case, I've always believed that it's not what you have, but what you do with what you have that's important. We all have strengths and weaknesses. The ones who succeed use their strengths and don't let their weaknesses get them down. Anyway, that's my thought. What's yours?

Q. *What is bulimia?*

With the estimates of eating disorders running as high as 10 percent of teenage girls and increasing among boys, we may very well be living in the age of eating disorders. It is no coincidence that we also live in an age obsessed with diets and model-like standards of beauty; images that we are bombarded with daily through all types of media and advertisement. At the same time we are a nation that is grossly overweight with poor eating habits exemplified by the fact that the average person gets 25 percent of his calories through French fries. When teenagers, who are already dealing with fragile egos and self-esteem, become obsessed with trying to conform to these often unrealistic standards, the result can be anorexia, bulimia (more often in girls), or steroid use and weight-lifting compulsion (more often in boys). Anorexia is a condition in which the teen thinks she is overweight even though she is actually critically underweight. Without intervention such teens actually starve themselves to death. These girls are typically perfectionists and high achievers who are plagued with low self-esteem. Bulimia differs from anorexia in that the teen compulsively binges on large quantities of high caloric food to satisfy a craving, and then purges herself of the despised calories by vomiting and often with laxatives. This process can cause dehydration, hormonal imbalance, depletion of minerals, and damage to the organs. Although you will want to inform your child or teen about these risks, it is more important to encourage them to pursue a healthy diet and reasonable weight goals. For example:

A. Well, now that you know the problem, I also want you to know the solution. The key is to eat reasonably healthy food, exercise, and learn to accept that few of us are going to look like a beauty queen or hunk of the year. And *none* of us is ever going to be perfect. Part of being happy in this life is learning what's important and what just seems important. Having a great body can seem important because of all the hype that we see on the media and all the attention that people like that do get. But if having a great body really made people happy, then Marilyn Monroe and thousands of other great-looking people wouldn't have been so miserable. A better goal is to have a *healthy* body. That means not eating a lot of junk food and getting too heavy, but also not dieting and trying to be perfect, either. And it also means staying physically active your whole life. If you always have a sport or exercise routine, then it's a lot easier to keep your weight right and to stay attractive.

Q. *Why did this have to happen to us?*

When unwanted challenges strike a family, it is typical to wonder why this has happened. Young kids may think that they are bad and are being punished. You want to reassure them that this is not the case. But all kids need to know that life is filled with unexpected challenges and that handling such challenges can help make a person or a family stronger. There are many ways to get this point through. One of our favorites is in the form of a story:

A. I know it can feel so unfair when something like this happens. We didn't do anything to deserve this, but still, such things happen and are a part of life. Life gives us undeserved breaks sometimes and sometimes it gives us undeserved challenges. The secret, though, is not what you get, but what you do with what you get. Let me tell you a story and see what you get from it:

There was once a brother and a sister (make this fit your own situation, for example, two brothers) who lived near a beautiful mountain. One day their parents asked them if they felt ready to climb the mountain together. The kids liked the challenge and agreed to give it a try. As the day of the big climb approached, they felt a little nervous. Maybe they weren't ready to make the climb. What if they couldn't do it? Their parents encouraged them to do their best and see what happened. And so the family set out to climb the mountain together. After some time they reached a steep part of the mountain that was covered with rocks. The younger of the kids became worried and said, "How can we climb this, it's all covered with rocks." One of the parents put an arm on the child's shoulder and replied, "It's okay. The rocks are what we climb on."

A Brief Review

Disabilities refer to difficulties with physical, emotional, intellectual, or social development and affect millions of parents and children. It is important for parents to become knowledgeable about the disability or chronic illness, to understand their legal rights, and to get to know their children's teachers and other professionals who can help. Children with disabilities and chronic illness not only need to cope with the particular challenges of their condition, but also need support in building courage and self-esteem. When disability or chronic illness strikes a family, whether through a parent or a child, it is a challenge that can make the family stronger or weaker, depending on how it is handled.

Chapter 11

Money and Work

Melanie couldn't believe all the credit card applications. Her first year away at college and suddenly she was being treated as a valued customer by some of the biggest banks in the country. Cool. College was going to be even more fun than she had expected. Of course she would be careful. She had heard about kids getting into trouble with credit cards, but that had not been something she was afraid of.

But then she saw that dress she just had to have. And of course the shoes. What good is a killer dress without matching shoes? And what about the purse that went so perfectly with the outfit? After all, who was it that once said that it was the human ability to accessorize that separated us from the lower animals? Probably Leonardo de Gucci or somebody like that. Anyway, a few hundred dollars wasn't going to kill anyone. Her parents had always provided for her, and things had a way of working out.

Of course that was before spring break. How could she not go with her friends to the beach, even if she had spent her monthly allowance already? That's when she was really glad she had the cards. Where else was she going to come up with that kind of money? Get a job? Not a chance. Her parents had always believed that she should enjoy her youth, because there would be plenty of time for work later. Not that she had any idea about what kind of work she would eventually do. Nothing that she could think of doing seemed like much fun. Her parents worked boring jobs, it seemed to her, and life was just too short for that.

The call from her dad really surprised her. How did the credit card company even know how to contact him? She hadn't heard him this angry since that time she sneaked the car out when she was fifteen and her friend got that lousy bump on her forehead when she hit that ice patch. You'd think that her bill was a million dollars the way he acted—threatening to pull her out of school and make her get a job and yelling about how irresponsible she was. Ha! If he thinks this is bad, just wait until he hears from the other two credit card companies.

What Parents Need to Know

First, don't wait until your child goes off to college to begin teaching the importance of money and work. Worse, don't leave the job up to their future spouse or the creditors. Getting through about the relative importance of work and money is too important to leave to chance. How important? Money issues are ranked the number one stressor for most people in our society. Furthermore, this is true at almost *all* levels of income. This is pretty amazing when you consider that most of us think that our money worries would be over if we could just earn another X amount of dollars a year. The truth, however, is that our lifestyle just expands with the additional income, keeping the chains of consumerism tight as we slave away to keep up with our never-ending appetite for more stuff.

The first step in teaching our children how to handle money and work responsibly is to get a handle on our own spending—which means getting a handle on our own desires. This is tough in a society that bombards us daily with clever and persuasive advertising and merchandizing depicting an endless supply of wonderful things and experiences to purchase. Nonetheless, the real solution to the money/stress dilemma is not to earn more but to want less. Or if you are *not* a saint, then at least consider moving in that direction.

Know Your Values

What values do you want to get through to your children and teens about work and money? Do you want them to see work as a noble contribution that we each make to the common welfare or something you just do to earn as much money as you can? If you don't want them to see work as constant drudgery or minimally satisfying, then teach them how various jobs are important in the scheme of things. Teach them the value of doing a job well and taking pride in the outcome whether it is a successful heart surgery or a well-dug ditch. And help them listen for their calling, that wonderful passion that can truly give a career meaning and satisfaction. Too few people obtain that level of work fulfillment, but it is a goal worth pursuing.

What about money? Do you want them to value money as a measure of self-worth or as a means to providing a secure lifestyle with opportunities that might otherwise be unavailable? Perhaps you would be okay if they did not value it at all or if they worshipped it as the essence of happiness. Unfortunately, the world has always had a large share of wealthy and miserable people who thought that money was more important than job satisfaction and human relationships. And there have been many more who have found that poverty could be just as miserable.

Maybe you want to get through that money is important, but that what you do to earn it is even more important. Beyond earning enough money to pay for the necessities of life plus some recreation and entertainment, finding a career or job that matches one's talents and gives a person a way to be creative and productive is much more likely to add to that person's happiness than earning more dollars. Finding a career or job that leaves time to build strong relationships with children, spouse, and friends will do the same. What do you really want for yourself and your children?

Spending Speaks Louder Than Words

Whatever your values, your children will know them from how you spend your time and money. Your words will become like so much background static while the clear picture of your actions communicates with brilliant clarity. If you say that you value education, but spend your free time and money on recreation and entertainment, what message gets through? If you say that work is important, but you constantly cut corners and do not give it your best, what do your children learn about the value of hard work and a job well done? If you advocate that money is not the measure of a person's worth, but you constantly talk about how much people make and are awed by personal wealth, what gets through? If you tell your kids to be responsible, but constantly hand out money to them according to their whims or yours, then what do they really learn about handling money?

Think about how you spend your time and money, especially as it relates to your children. Then, if you see inconsistencies between what you believe and what you do, make some changes to bring them into alignment. This will enable you to send a single message that is both clear and powerful to your children.

What Kids Need to Know

Start teaching your children how to manage money while they are young. The best way to do this is to give them practical experience. A young child of five can be shown various prices of things on a trip to the grocery store. Give her a dollar and let her pick out something that she wants to spend it on. Teach her about saving as a form of collecting. She can "collect" pennies, nickels, dimes, and so forth as a way of getting used to the idea. As kids get older, there is nothing better for teaching them how to handle money responsibly than an allowance.

Allowances

Responsible money management is about making good choices. Learning early that a choice to buy something is also a choice not to have that money to buy something else can help a child throughout his life. Without an allowance, your child must constantly come to you for anything that he wants or needs money to provide. While this may teach him how to negotiate or beg, it does not teach him how to manage money. Plus, when your child has an allowance, you can avoid those annoying little money-grubbing hassles while getting to say those wonderful magical words "That's what your allowance is for."

A good rule of thumb is to give a child between fifty cents and a dollar for each year of age as an allowance. This money is not to be tied to chores, because you do not want him to learn that helping out with his own home is something for which he has to be paid. Nor should it be "taken away" as a punishment. This money is just his to spend, as he wants. The only limit that you want to place on this spending is if it violates health, safety, or your family values.

As kids get older you can increase the allowance to cover such items that you would otherwise dole out money to provide, such as lunch money and even a clothing allowance. You may also want to encourage giving to charity by including an additional amount that is to be donated to the charity of your child's choice each week. To encourage your child to delay gratification and learn to save, start with a piggy bank of some sort and then later take him to open up a savings account at a bank. Teach him about interest. Older kids can also be taught how to invest in mutual funds or directly into the stock market. Some investment companies now offer kid-friendly funds that include stocks of companies kids know and like. Make sure that your child knows that he can make withdrawals whenever he wants or he will see savings as a black hole from which money never returns. Instead of prohibiting withdrawals, talk to her about saving up for more expensive items that are special. You can help her set savings goals for such things and even offer to match her savings until the goal is reached.

An added benefit of an allowance is that it can be used to help teach children that actions sometimes have economic consequences. For example, without an allowance when a child throws a ball through a window, she might get a lecture or sent to her room. With an allowance, she gets a lesson in the cost of window repair and is expected to help pay for the damage. ("Help" as opposed to paying for the entire repair, unless she is independently wealthy.) When a child forgets to do his chores, instead of a scolding, he has to pay the person who does it for him a predetermined fee. These practical economic lessons get through much louder than lectures for most kids.

Teach Your Child to Make Friends With Work

Work is a part of life that can bring joy or misery. Much of the difference is one of attitude. Teaching our children that work is valuable and rewarding for its own sake, and not just a means to earn money, can be a wonderful gift. The following tips can help you instill an appreciation for doing "an honest day's work" and reaping the satisfaction work can bring.

Tips for Building a Positive Work Ethic

1. **Encourage your child's efforts with schoolwork.** School is your child's first "job" and can set the stage for whatever follows. Point out the positives with such phrases as: "I like this work"; "Nice job with this. You really did some good work"; "I like how hard you are working"; "Your hard work really paid off on that test"; "This is very interesting."

2. **Encourage your child to work with you around the house.** Chores are a great way to teach responsibility for work. To get off on the right foot, teach young children how to do chores by working together. Start with chores that are fun, such as run-

ning the vacuum cleaner or folding the towels (well, they are fun to kids, anyway). As you work together, be generous with your encouragement, saying such attitude-building comments as: "You are doing such a nice job with this"; "It feels good to do a good job, doesn't it?"; "I sure appreciate your help"; "You are really a good worker." As your child gets older and takes on more responsibility, continue to look for ways to encourage the effort and the result. Show him what is expected and make sure that he follows through.

3. **Read books together about careers.** Help your child begin developing a wide frame of reference for work through reading together and talking about various types of work. Ask about these careers with questions like: "What do you think it would be like to be a marine biologist?" "That sure sounds like an exciting career to me. What do you think?" "He sure seemed to enjoy his work. Why do you think he did?" Don't forget to include parenting as a career. Many women (and men) still choose this essential career as their only job. Others prefer to pursue both a parenting career and a job that pays a salary. Your own values, as always, will come into play on this issue. However, it is important to stress the importance of parenting as an essential job in our community, and one that, like all jobs, requires education and training to do well.

4. **Take advantage of "take your child to work" days.** Give your kids opportunities to see the adult world of work in action. Take them with you to work and talk about what you do. Keep it positive, focusing on the things that bring you satisfaction. Although it is also good to point out that there are parts of any job that are less desirable, you want to use this time to make a positive impression. Follow up by talking about your

work at dinner or at other times with your child. Again, be positive, and when you talk about problems, make sure that you talk about solutions as well.

5. **Encourage kids to start a business or get a job.** Kids derive a lot of satisfaction from earning extra money. Many a successful entrepreneur started out with a lemonade stand or a shoeshine business. As kids get older, baby-sitting and yard work are great ways to earn and learn. Make sure that they do not just focus on the money by talking about how responsible they are and how much good their work is doing. Finally, do not let these jobs interfere with schoolwork. Money is immediate, and can become very seductive, but school opens up many more career opportunities in the long run. It is up to parents to set limits on how many hours a child or teen can work. Besides keeping a close eye on grades, a good rule of thumb is no more than twenty hours a week of outside work even for older teens.

QUESTIONS KIDS SOMETIMES ASK (AND POSSIBLE ANSWERS)

(YOUNG CHILDREN)

Q. *What do you do for a living?*

Children will wonder what their parents do to earn a living, and telling them provides a good opportunity to encourage a positive outlook toward work. Remember the importance of relevancy to children. So instead of saying that "Mommy is a financial analyst for a major banking institution," be a little more descriptive and say, "Mommy helps banks run better." As the child gets older, go into more details and offer to take her with you to see for herself.

A. I am a teacher. I teach fourth grade. One of the things that I really like about this job is that I get to be with children, and I really like children. Plus, I get to help them learn. And I get to learn new things myself. I think that's what makes for a good job: being able to learn and having something that makes a difference to others. I hope that you find a job some day that makes you feel good inside, too.

Q. *Why doesn't Mommy have a job?*

When one parent works outside the home and the other stays home, whether mother or father, kids will eventually wonder why. Share your family values with them. For example:

A. I do have a job, a very important job. Do you know what it is? My job is to help take care of our family. Daddy and I decided that it was more important for me to stay home to help you and your sister and him than it was to earn extra money. I like having time to read with you and play with you and to cook dinner and make cookies together and all that other good stuff that I wouldn't have time to do if I had to go away to work every day. Maybe when you get older, I'll go back to that kind of job again. Do you know what I did before you were born?

(OLDER CHILDREN AND TEENS)

Q. *Why don't we ever have enough money to do stuff?*

When a family struggles financially, it can be difficult to explain to the children. The key is to avoid becoming defensive. Address their frustrations head-on with empathy. Let them know what the situation is and what you are doing about it. And take the opportunity to communicate that beyond the basics, happiness is not dependent on things that money can buy.

A. I know you get tired of hearing that things are too expensive or "we can't afford that right now." Sometimes we feel the same way, too. And I know that it's tough to see some of the other kids who have things that you want, but that we can't afford to give you. Fortunately, we have always had food to eat, a roof over our heads and clothing to wear. A lot of kids can't say that today, even in America, much less in poorer countries. I don't know if this will matter much right now, but the things that are really important don't cost money. Having a family that loves you and pulls together; having good friends; doing good work, even if it doesn't pay that great; these are the things that make life worth living. And if you count those things as much as we do, then we're all very rich around here.

Q. *Why did Dad (Mom) lose his (her) job?*

A straightforward answer is usually the best way to answer this when circumstances beyond your control are the cause. Besides the information, this is a good chance to demonstrate how you keep your head up when life throws you a curveball. For example:

A. Our company wasn't making as much money as we used to, and they had to lay off some people to keep expenses down. I was in a group of 150 people who got laid off. It's pretty disappointing, but it happens. I've already started looking for a new job and plan to keep looking until I find one. In the meantime, we may be a little tight on money and have to do without some things. I know I can count on all of you to help out until things get back to normal.

Let's say that losing your job was not due to circumstances, but that you did something that caused you to be let go. This is a more sensitive matter, but one that you should also answer honestly, if for no other reason than you do not want your child to hear the truth from somebody else and find out that you misled her. As always, you do not necessarily have to tell her the whole truth. If there are details that might shock or otherwise be hard for her to understand, you can keep your answer general but honest. However detailed you choose to get, use this opportunity to help your child learn from your mistakes. Your courage in sharing may help her avoid a similar one herself someday.

A. I made a mistake. My new supervisor and I have not seen eye to eye for some time. Last week she told me to do something that is not part of my job, and I told her flat out that I wouldn't do it. She told me to do it or look for another job, and I guess I lost my temper. I said some things in anger and stormed out. She fired me. I think my mistake was letting my feelings for her get in the way of my better judgment. I know that in a small company that there is no such thing as "not my job." Everyone has to pitch in and do whatever needs to be done. I just didn't like the way she talked to me, kind of disrespectful. Still, I should have tried to work it out or else begun looking for a new job. There was no excuse for losing my temper like that.

Q. *What can I do to earn some money?*

Encouraging your kids' initiative is a way to build long-term motivation for work. Even if they don't ask, you can suggest this at a time when they want more than they can afford from their allowance. Avoid the mind-set of the parent in the opening vignette who thought that childhood should be a time of fun, safe from the worries of work. To a kid, earning money for work is fun, and it can become a lifelong habit.

A. Say, I'm really glad to hear you thinking that way. It shows initiative. I can think of a couple of personal things that you can do for me if you'd like. I'd pay you to shine my shoes and wash the car. Of course, you'd have to finish your family chores first. If you want to do some things outside of home, we can brainstorm some ideas. What are some ideas that you have?

Q. *Why do I have to give some of my money to charity?*

If you want your children to learn to be givers as well as earners, then it's good to start early. Add a portion to their allowance for giving, but then insist that this money be given away charitably, and not saved or spent for personal use. Some families use a "three jar" system. This idea literally separates allowance into three jars: one for spending, one for saving and one for giving. You can proportion the money into thirds, or divide it however you and your child agree. Just be sure to address the "why" of giving to make your answer as relevant as possible. For example:

A. Remember that we discussed adding some money to your allowance for giving? I know it is sometimes hard to give money to others when there are things that we still want for ourselves. But maybe that's what makes giving even more meaningful—when it requires some sacrifice. It takes a big person to make a sacrifice for others—especially others that she does not even know. That's part of being part of a community. We give to help those who need a little extra help to make it or to those groups that support the good work and values that can make our community and world a better place. For example, you seem very interested in the environment. Why don't we look into some of the groups that work to protect our environment? Would you like to go online with me and see what we can find?

A Brief Review

Helping our children learn to manage money responsibly and prepare for the world of work is an ongoing process. First, it involves knowing one's own values regarding money and work, and then deciding what you want for your children. Remembering that how we spend our time and money communicates these values louder than our words, we want to set an example that is consistent with what we want to teach. We can use allowances to help our children learn about money management, being sure to encourage saving and giving, as well as spending. Finally, encouraging a positive attitude about work and helping our children learn about various career opportunities can give them a leg up on this important aspect of life.

Chapter 12

Sexuality . . .
the mysterious gift

It was a typical teen party—typical in the sense that the hostess's parents were out of town and there were no adults around to get in the way. The word of the party had spread like wildfire along the Internet as teen after teen had forwarded the simple E-mail invitation to friends. This was definitely a party not to be missed for one reason and one reason only: There were no parents around to get in the way. To Melissa, the hostess, this meant that her popularity was about to take a huge jump. To her friends, and about a hundred other kids she either barely knew or who were total strangers to her, this meant alcohol, other drugs, and sex.

Around midnight, with the party in full force and the house becoming trashed to the tune of about $20,000, Jared, a sixteen-year-old sophomore, was escorting his slightly intoxicated fourteen-year-old girlfriend, Sara, to one of the upstairs bedrooms. They had been dating about a month now, and he was ready for something more than making out. He figured she was still a virgin, but with her body he didn't think that would last long. Besides, sex was no big deal these days, and he was in the mood for some fun.

A half hour later she still had her clothes on, and he was finding this a lot harder than he expected. She had been happy to make out as usual and had not protested when he put a hormone-driven hand under her top and massaged her breasts. But when he had tried to take off her shorts, she had moved his hand away and said that she was staying a virgin. "Why?" he now asked, his voice registering more than annoyance, almost contempt for such a notion.

"I don't know. I guess I'm just not ready for sex," she said defensively, thinking about how she had been the envy of all her friends when Jared, one of the acknowledged cool kids in the school, had asked her out.

After another fifteen minutes of Jared's rationalizing, cajoling, and threatening to break off the relationship, he had unbuttoned her shorts and worked a hand down to where she knew it was just a matter of time before he tried to put something else. "I told you I wasn't ready for sex," she said a little more firmly, moving his hand away from her. "What if I just give you a blow job?"

What Parents Need to Know

Perhaps you are feeling shocked or appalled at the scenario mentioned above. Unfortunately this scene is not so far removed or even unusual in this day and age. Sexuality at the beginning of the twenty-first century is in a state of flux. Even among the mainstream there is very little unifying philosophy or morality that governs behavior beyond such basic taboos as incest, rape, and child abuse. Attitudes and values governing consensual sexual behavior seem to range from very conservative to kinky to the point of satire. Sexuality continues to be a "hot" medium for advertising and entertainment so that we are constantly bombarded with titillating images of men, women, and even teenagers clad in provocative clothing designed to attract and arouse viewers, and by association, build a loyal following. Movies, TV, music, and the Internet present a wide variety of sexually charged material including recreational sex, romantic sexuality, spiritual lovemaking, and even violent and abusive encounters. Adults themselves seem confused about sexuality with marriage rates still high and rates of infidelity and divorce almost as high. In fact, the Bill Clinton–Monica Lewinsky sex scandal revealed that we are no longer even sure what constitutes "sexual relations." No wonder that an increasing number of young teenage girls no longer consider oral sex as anything more than foreplay.

Yet most of us would agree that sexuality is a gift—a wonderful, exciting aspect of life that has the power to generate emotional closeness, intense pleasure, and bonds that can last a lifetime. We want our children to know this wonderful side of their sexuality and to become emotionally whole, responsible, loving, intimate people who form meaningful relationships that not only fulfill themselves and their loved one, but also in due time (and here's the best part) give us grandchildren!

Helping them navigate through the treacherous waters of adolescence while trying to make sense of their emerging sexuality is challenging for at least three reasons: First, sexuality continues to be complexly wrapped up with human intimacy and relationships. Even those proponents of open marriages and "free love" back in the seventies came to understand that although one could build a good case for "free love" intellectually, the reality was that most people are far too possessive and/or loyal to handle it emotionally. Even those who *could* handle this freedom emotionally found that their relationships were constantly changing as new sexual objects appeared on one or the other's radar screens signaling the "time to move on." This does not lead to stable marriages, communities, or societies.

The second issue is that you may have noticed that human sexuality continues to be complexly wrapped up with human reproduction. Although a million teen pregnancies a year suggest that many people have forgotten this fact, and though the reality of human cloning looms on the horizon, reproduction is still the number one reason nature decided that sexuality should be so pleasurable. Or as it says in the Bible: "Go forth and multiply." Five billion people in the world later, it seems that we have multiplied perhaps too well. Teaching our children the responsibilities and obligations of bringing children into the world is more than just a matter of telling them about the birds and bees.

Third, sexuality has become even more dangerous. While rape, violence over who loves or betrays whom, complications of childbirth, and sexually transmitted diseases (STDs) have dogged humankind from the beginning, we now live in the era of AIDS, an incurable STD that is ravaging parts of the world and threatening the rest. In the United States some twenty-thousand teenagers a year contract the HIV virus that inevitably produces AIDS and causes death. Three million more teens contract some form of STDs a year. Many experts attribute this to teens feeling invincible, the same erroneous belief that underlies many auto fatalities, alcohol and other drug abuse, and violence.

It is clear that sexuality is a high-stakes proposition. The attitudes, values, and beliefs that our kids form about this subject will not only have life-and-death consequences but, perhaps even more important, will affect the overall quality of that life profoundly. What kids hear from other kids and through the media will be a huge influence—often an inaccurate or unwelcome influence. Parents can counteract this influence by using the communication skills and other means suggested throughout this book to get through to their children and teens on a frequent basis.

What Kids Need to Know About Sexuality

Two of the greatest challenges of adolescence are to accept one-self as a sexual being and to develop a philosophy of life by which to live. As important as these goals are, we do not have to wait until our kids are teenagers to begin preparing them for these tasks. Giving children good information while strengthening their core values all along the way can set a strong foundation that will translate to positive behavior later. While it is beyond the scope of this book (or the nerve of the authors) to tell you what to teach your children about sexuality, there are at least two broad areas that kids need to know about:

1. **Becoming a sexual being.** Most parents want their children to grow up with a healthy appreciation and enjoyment of their sexuality so that they will be personally fulfilled and capable of bringing joy and fulfillment to their partners someday. We can begin with young children by naming the body parts. When giving a child a bath, name the various body parts from nose to toes and everything in between, including the penis or vagina. Let your child know that boys have penises and girls have vaginas. You can also teach young children that they have some control over what they do with their bodies. For example, if they do not want to give Aunt Beck a big kiss, especially when she always goes for the lips, they may abstain. This right to say no will almost certainly come in handy later. At about age eight you can begin discussing the incredible

mystery of reproduction with them. You can wait until they are a little older if you want, but by then it won't be much of a mystery anymore, because they will have already heard about it from the kid down the street with the older sibling, and you will be spending most of your time correcting misinformation.

Another valuable lesson is to teach your kids to delay gratification. Do they want a new video player? Fine, but don't rush out to buy it today. Teach them to save their allowance for it or wait until a birthday or the holiday season. Learning self-restraint is a powerful lesson for later when raging hormones want to propel them into immediate gratification. Once your kids do begin adolescence and these incredible hormonal changes affect everything from mood to body shape and size, hair growth, reproductive organs, and the emergence of sexual desire, teens need to know that this is natural, normal, and good.

Teens also need to know that they do not have to look like the models they see in the media to be attractive sexual beings. With eating disorders among teen girls and steroid use among boys still major problems, it is important for kids to learn to like their bodies without their bodies having to be perfect. We also want them to enjoy their feelings of sexual awakening without shame. At the same time we want to remind them that they can postpone gratification, not act on every desire or impulse, and have the right, sometimes the *obligation*, to say no to themselves and to pushy peers.

2. **The facts and values of life.** We recommend that whenever you talk to your kids about the facts of life that you also talk about the values of life that are associated with them. Of course, these values, and to some extent what facts you choose to

emphasize, will be determined by your own beliefs, religious and otherwise. Be sure to discuss the specifics of reproduction (including how the sperm gets to the egg . . . and not like one parent did when she explained that in the middle of the night the sperm crawled out of Daddy, across the bed and into Mommy!) Also be sure to cover birth control and STDs and how to prevent them. There are many good books written for kids that can help you cover this. You may also want to check to see if you child's school or pediatrician has material that will be helpful.

TIPS FOR TALKING WITH YOUR KIDS
ABOUT THE FACTS AND VALUES OF LIFE

Having the guts to talk with your kids about this subject is a good start. To increase the probability that your message will get through, keep these tips in mind:

1. **Clarify your own values.** Take some time to think about your own values regarding sexuality and what you hope for your children. Remember that they probably will not adopt your values 100 percent, but since clarity leads to power, the clearer you can be, the better chance you will have of influencing them. Some of these values might include the following: avoid hurting others; avoid hurting yourself; honesty; caring about feelings—yours and others; self-restraint; assertiveness; love and intimacy. If you are married or have a partner, talk this over together and decide what you will share with your child.

2. **Talk early; talk often.** Don't wait to have a big talk about the birds and the bees. Instead, look for opportunities to talk

about sexuality throughout your child's life. The more often you reinforce your message, the better chance it will take. Watching TV or movies together offers many opportunities to talk about both the facts and values of sexuality, and to correct messages that go against your values. Turn off the tube after the show and then talk.

3. **Keep your talks age appropriate.** It is best to be matter-of-fact when talking about the facts of life so that your kids get the idea that sexuality is a normal part of life and not some big secret. Still, consider your child's age when deciding how much to tell them and what words to use. For example, if a four-year-old asks, "Where do babies come from?" you might reply simply, "Mommy and Daddy make a baby together. It grows inside Mommy's tummy until it's ready to be born." If your eight-year-old asks, you will want to take the opportunity to go into the whole nine yards from sperm and egg to delivery. Also keep in mind that some kids are more inquisitive than others and will ask more questions. How much you tell at an early age depends on your own comfort level and how mature you think that your child is.

4. **Talk to kids of either sex.** A lot of parents prefer to talk with only the child of their own sex about this subject. This misses a good opportunity to model the act of talking with the opposite sex about sexuality, a skill that is missing in too many marriages. When possible, it is useful for both parents to talk with the child together. You can reinforce each other and play off each other's ideas.

5. **Talk with one child at a time.** This is not a hard-and-fast rule, but often when you try talking with two or more children

about sexuality, the whole thing becomes hysterically amusing to them and you get nowhere. This is probably a defense against the discomfort of the subject. A child alone, however, will work through his discomfort if you stay calm yourself and remain focused on your message. In fact, they will often have a "Wow!" experience.

6. **Use resources.** Whether you give a child a book to read and then discuss, read it together and discuss as you go, or talk first and give them a book to read afterwards then follow-up later, is a matter of personal choice. However, we strongly recommend that you get a book, video, or other resources to help you cover all the information that you want to cover. This will take pressure off you to remember everything and it will give you the added credibility of a book or other resource. Also, keep your eyes open for current events in the papers, TV, or even movies that can make for useful discussion. For example, when one community found that they had an unusually high incidence of STDs, it was traced to wild sex parties in which teens had multiple partners in a single night. The local PBS station did an excellent special on the subject, complete with a town hall meeting and follow-up discussion. This was an excellent show to watch with a teen or preteen and then discuss based on previous talks about the risks of sexuality, as well as the values you want to reinforce.

7. **Stay calm and don't be afraid to laugh.** While you do want to communicate that sexuality is a serious subject, it is also a joyful subject. A little bit of laughter can break the ice and keep the tone from getting too heavy. Try to keep a natural, conversational tone that leaves the door open for follow-up questions and talks at any time.

Questions Kids Sometimes Ask (and Possible Answers)

Because kids will not always ask, take the initiative and address these questions anyway. Your answers, of course, will depend on your own values and spiritual beliefs. In some of these sample answers we have included references to God. In others we have not. This, again, is for illustration only, and your own beliefs should be expressed when you talk with your children.

Young Children (Ages Two to Five)

Q. *Where do babies come from?*
We addressed this earlier, but since it is a classic, here is a simple, straightforward answer:

A. Mommy and Daddy make a baby with the help of God. It grows inside Mommy's tummy until it is ready to be born and then comes out.

Q. *Why don't I have a penis like Chad does?*
This needs to be addressed because some girls will think that they once had a penis, but that it fell off, and some boys will be afraid that it could fall off.

A. Because you are a girl and girls have a vagina instead of a penis. That's one of the things that make boys and girls different.

Q. *Why do I have to wear clothes?*

A. Remember when we talked about how girls have vaginas and boys have penises? These are our private parts. *Private* means just for us. We don't show them to other people, except sometimes when Mommy and Daddy are giving you a bath or when you visit the doctor.

OLDER CHILDREN AND PRETEENS

Q. *Where do babies come from?*

A. Babies begin to be created when something called "sperm" that comes from inside a man fertilizes the egg inside a woman. When the two come together at the right time, a miracle happens and a new life begins to grow. As this new life gets bigger, it is called a fetus. It takes about nine months for this fetus to grow into a baby that is ready to be born. When the baby is ready, the woman usually goes to the hospital and the baby is delivered through her vagina.

Q. *How does the sperm get inside the woman?*

This is the big question. And if your child does not already know, the answer is likely to shock him. Just keep your tone calm and reassure him that it is okay to feel shocked if he does, but that sexuality is a very normal part of life. This is also a good opportunity to share your values about sexual activity and to begin building a connection between sexuality and intimacy.

A. That is a very good question. Do you already know the answer? (Said with a smile.) Have you ever heard of "sexual intercourse" or "making love"? These are terms that describe a very special activity between two people. When a man and a woman love each other very much and decide that they want to start a family, they sometimes "make love." This involves a lot of hugging and kissing and being very close. The part that makes the baby is when the man puts his penis inside the woman's vagina and releases some fluid that carries the sperm. If they are lucky, then one of these sperm finds the egg and they unite. This eventually grows into a baby. Pretty amazing, huh?

Q. *What is oral sex?*

This question became pretty popular during the Clinton impeachment proceedings, as prime-time news felt no compunction about using the term in front of America's children. Now, with so many young teens acting as if oral sex were no big deal, it is up to parents to discuss this and share your own values. If you have not talked about sexual intercourse and other matters before this question arises, and if your child is eight or older, then take it from the top. Do not begin with oral sex, but lead up to it gradually. If your child is less than eight, or less mature, then give a partial answer that will hold her until she is older. For example:

A.1. That is something that grown-ups sometimes do when they love each other and want to be close.

If they are older and somewhat knowledgeable, then you might try this approach:

A.2. Do you have any idea what it means? (This is always a good opening, because kids will often have a vague idea that you can build on. If they don't, or resist sharing, just go on with your explanation.) Well, there are two words: *Oral*, which refers to the mouth; and *sex*, which refers to intimate physical contact between two people—usually involving the genitals. In other words, it's a very intimate and personal form of sexual activity that involves using the mouth to give pleasure to a partner's penis or vagina. At this point you will probably get a "yuck" response of some kind. If so, use your own values to determine what to say next. If you are comfortable with oral sex, then you might say something like: I know, it sounds pretty gross right now. It is also something that is very personal and should be saved for when . . . again, fill in the blank here according to your values. For example, a) "you really love someone very deeply"; b) "you are married"; c) "you want to be sexually intimate without risking pregnancy." If you oppose oral sex under any conditions, then you can easily build on you child's response by saying something like:) Although a lot of people accept this as a normal part of adult sexuality, we do not. We believe _____.

Q. *What is a homosexual?*

This is important to bring up for the obvious sexual reasons, but also because it is important to teach kids tolerance for people who are different from them. Whether you believe that homosexuality is a choice or the way some people are genetically programmed, go beyond that message and get through to your kids about the rights of all people to be treated respectfully.

A. Usually, men fall in love with women and women with men, and they are sexually attracted to the opposite sex. Some people, though, fall in love with people of the same sex and are sexually attracted to them. When it's a guy, he is sometimes referred to as homosexual or gay. When it's a woman, she is sometimes referred to as lesbian. Some people seem to be able to fall in love with and are sexually attracted to either sex, and are called bisexual. The important thing to know is that whatever a person's sexual attraction, he or she is just as worthwhile as anyone else, and that nobody should ever tease or make fun of someone because of this. In fact if you hear someone being cruel to someone who is gay, I hope you'll have the courage to stand up and say stop.

Q. *How do you become gay?*

A. We don't know for sure, but most people who are attracted to the same sex seem to have been born that way, just like most people who are heterosexual—that means being attracted to the opposite sex—are born that way. There may be others who are more bisexual and become gay out of their experiences. But we also know that it is very difficult to change a person's sexual orientation. So, you can't "catch" being gay like a cold from a teacher or someone else who happens to be gay.

Q. *What would you do if you found out that I was gay?*

This may be a test question to check out if you are safe to share concerns about sexual orientation. You want to reassure your child that you will still love and accept him or her no matter what. Then, depending on your own beliefs, you would talk about your course of action. The following answer is a good start for someone who believes that same-sex attraction is okay, but if your child is concerned, you will want to get more information from one of the Web sites in the resource chapter or through a counselor who is trained in this area.

A. Well, the first thing is that I would keep on loving you just as much as I do now. We would talk about whether you wanted to keep this private or "come out" as the term goes. Even though society has become much more open and accepting about same-sex attraction, it can still be a challenge, especially for a teenager. So, we might also arrange to talk with a counselor about how to help you handle things emotionally. However, I think you should know that there is a lot of confusion among teenagers about whether they really are attracted to the same sex or the opposite sex. In fact, in one study, 25 percent of eighth graders were unsure, even though only about 2 percent of them were really gay. By the time they were tenth graders, though, only 5 percent were unsure. Sexuality is a complicated area, and it takes time to really sort it out. Do you wonder if you are gay?

TEENS

All of the previous questions will apply to teens, as well. The following questions can be answered for preteens if they ask. If they don't ask, then you can wait until they are young teenagers.

Q. *What is okay to do sexually when you are on a date?*

Most parents dodge this question and just focus on when it's okay to have sexual intercourse. This doesn't help the teen enough in determining her code of behavior. Because your own values will determine what to share with your teen, the following answer leaves room for variation according to how liberal or conservative you feel about the subject. Keep in mind that the average age of sexual activity today is between fifteen and sixteen, which most of us view as too young.

A. I think it is really important that you wait until _____ (Fill in the blank. For example: a) You are out of high school; b) you are an adult; c) you are married.) before you become fully active sexually. And then, I hope it is with someone _____ (a. who is very special to you; b) that you love deeply) because sharing that part of yourself with someone you care about deeply, and not just using sex for recreation, makes it stay special. (Again, your own values may change this last line). But, I also know that teenagers are anxious to experience their sexuality. So, what I want you to agree to is that you will limit yourself to _____ (for example, kissing and hugging, dancing and exploring with your clothes on). And again, only with someone you really care about. Then, to help keep your hormones from taking over completely, I think we should talk about masturbation. (Be ready for an eye roll here.) Seriously, I know this is uncomfortable territory, but we want you to know how we feel about it. If your religious values prohibit masturbation, then make sure your teen knows this. Otherwise, you want to dispel any potential guilt that they will feel from doing something that almost all teens do to relieve sexual tension. For example: One thing about masturbation is that it relieves sexual tension without violating your values. It's a perfectly okay way to handle your sexual desires until you are _____ (older or married). Even so, it should be limited to when you really feel a strong build-up of sexual tension, and not just used to relieve boredom or get a daily dose of excitement.

Note: If you have conservative values regarding your teen's sexuality, then recognize that you are traveling upstream against a very strong current of sexuality coming from within your teen as well as from society at large. To effectively get your values through in this atmosphere, you will almost certainly need help. A particularly powerful form of help can come from a religious youth group that supports conservative values. When teens decide that delaying sexual activity until marriage is the right thing to do (perhaps even the "cool" thing to do), then they support each other in this challenge. In addition, it is likely that their parents are also promoting a conservative point of view. As any salmon will tell you, it is much easier to swim upstream with friends.

Q. *What should I do if my date pushes me to have sex?*

First, do not assume that a girl always asks this question. In today's teen world, girls are often the more sexually aggressive. However, because of size and strength, the real danger still lies with boys being aggressive with girls. It is important for parents of both sexes to talk to their kids before they begin dating about what is expected. There is far too much date violence among teens, including date rape. Parents of sons should insist that their sons understand that no means no—no matter what the girl intends it to mean. Find articles, movies, or TV shows that contain significant emotional experiences that show what happens when a guy pushes too hard and winds up in court on a date-rape charge. Parents of girls, on the other hand, need to address the "tease" issue. While being provocative and sexually inviting is absolutely no excuse for date rape, girls need to understand how to limit their risks in life, while still having a good time. Parents can role-play difficult situations and talk about how to handle them together. For example, "If you are at a party and you know the guy you are with has been drinking and he wants you to go upstairs with him to be alone together, what's he likely up to? What can you say to limit the risks?" Always remind your kids that whenever there is drinking, they should call you for a ride home with no consequences to them.

A.1. What can you think of to say?

A.2. One thing that I found was effective when I was young was . . .

A.3. I like that you are thinking ahead. Taking charge of your own body and not letting anyone else push you into something, especially sex, is very important. Let's talk about some ways that you can limit your risks and still have a good time. . . .

Q. *Did you have sex before you were married? How often?*
Gasp! That's the sound of air rushing out of your lungs, because this is one question that no parent really wants to be asked. There

are some good reasons for this: 1. If you were very conservative and waited until you were married and have been faithful ever since, sharing that information will probably at best have a neutral effect. More likely your kids will just write you off as having set impossibly high standards that they could never live up to anyway, so why try? 2. If you were, shall we say, more sexually liberal, then there is a good chance that you want your kids to be at least a tad more conservative. You correctly fear that giving them the juicy details of your life and times might also give them perceived permission to behave the same, if not more sexually. (Of course, if you believe that sex is there to be enjoyed with little restraint beyond health, safety, and basic human decency, then you have no problem with this question.) Remember back in chapter 1 that we suggested that you tell your child the truth, but not necessarily the whole truth. This means that you have a right to privacy, and this is a good time to assert it. One way to handle this is to tell them as much as you are comfortable with, and then plead the parental Fifth Amendment on the rest. For example:

A.1. Hmmm, that's a very personal question. Basically, I don't believe that parents should share the details of their sexual history with their children. But I will tell you this, I made a few mistakes that I quickly learned from. And what I learned is that sexuality is too precious a gift to be treated lightly. When you save it for someone that you really love, it can enhance that relationship and make it even more special. Now tell me, are you thinking about what to do about your own sexuality? (This is probably the real reason behind the question, and so you can probably skip the self-disclosure altogether and say . . .)

A.2. Hmmm, I see. Are you thinking about what to do about your own sexuality? (This can launch into a very useful discussion, especially if you stay warm, gentle, encouraging, and accepting.)

A Brief Review

Human sexuality continues to be both a mysterious gift as well as a challenge to solve in today's sexually charged world. Helping our children grow up with a positive attitude about their bodies and selves sets a good foundation for teaching both the facts of life and the values of life. Start talking when your kids are young about the information and beliefs that you want to encourage, making sure that you cover the vital information on reproduction, birth control, and STDs before they hit adolescence if at all possible. Then continue having talks whenever you have an opportunity, using such emotionally charged events as movies, television shows, and real-life situations as jumping-off points. Keep an encouraging and positive attitude to help keep the communication flowing, giving you opportunities to get through to your child's and teen's emerging philosophy of life.

Chapter 13

Tobacco . . .
piercing the smoke screen

Jason's mother sat him down at the dinner table one Saturday afternoon to a feast his eyes could not believe. In front of him were his three favorite desserts of all time. First was a death-by-chocolate sundae dripping with the most delicious-smelling hot fudge sauce he had ever smelled. Next to it was an equally delectable slice of coconut cream pie, an addiction for which he had long ago acquired. Finally, in the third spot, beckoning to him with a richness he could die for, was the biggest piece of German chocolate cake he had ever seen. German chocolate cake, in his understanding, was what we had fought two World Wars to win.

As Jason wondered what he had done to deserve such good fortune, his mother began to speak. "Son, what you see before you are your three most favorite desserts in the world. Is that correct?" Jason nodded, and drooled. His mother continued. "Now, I have some good news and some bad news for you. And then you get to make a decision." Jason's eyes shifted, a tad nervously. Something was up. "The good news is that you get to choose one of these three desserts to eat." So, that was it. He only got to eat one of them. Oh, well, he could live with that, he thought. "The bad news is that I have put poison in one of the three desserts. This poison is so lethal that it will kill you in a matter of minutes. It will be excruciatingly painful and there is no antidote. If you don't die from it immediately, then you will know that you have chosen wisely, or at least luckily. As your reward, you will be free to eat these desserts for the rest of your life with no concern of being poisoned."

Jason's mouth dropped open. "You're kidding, right?"

"No, sir," his mother replied firmly. "I'm dead serious. As serious as heart disease, lung disease, or cancer. Now which dessert do you choose? You have ten seconds to decide."

"This is crazy! I don't need ten seconds. Only an idiot would eat any of them now that you've messed them up."

"That's right," said his mother. "Only an idiot would take a one in three chance of eating poison, even for something that he really liked." She then took out a package of cigarettes and put them on the table. "So, tell me then. Why would a teenager ever start smoking these awful things when the odds of dying from heart disease, lung disease, or cancer is also one in three?"

Jason swallowed hard and wondered, "How did she find my cigarettes?"

What Parents Need to Know

The American Cancer Society reports that about three thousand teenagers a day try their first cigarette. And although the smoking rate has dropped during the past couple of years from 36 percent to 28 percent of all teens, that is still more than four million teenagers who are at risk of cutting their lives short or living with tobacco-related illness. In fact, the U.S. Centers for Disease Control and Prevention predict that one in three of them will die prematurely because of their smoking. That means that five million kids who are alive today will eventually die from smoking. Pretty scary statistics. Yet surprisingly easy to ignore.

The reason smoking risks are easy to ignore is that the most serious consequences of smoking do not usually happen for a long time. Imagine yourself sitting at a dinner party where the person sitting next to you begins to light up a cigarette, then turns and offers you one. Before you can answer you notice him rapidly losing weight. His cheeks hollow. His teeth yellow. His breath becomes putrid. An anguished moan escapes his lips as he falls over into his plate, dead from cancer. "No, thanks," you say. "I think I'll pass." Only an idiot, to quote the teenager in the opening vignette, would do otherwise. The problem with tobacco is not that it kills, but that it kills very slowly and intermittently. This gives us a chance to deny the consequences of our actions. This is especially true of teenagers, a group of individuals particularly gifted at denying that anything bad might ever happen to them. Part of our challenge as parents is to make these risks more real and more immediate. The mother in the opening story was attempting to get through by using the "poison sundae" metaphor. Later, when she and her son see someone smoking, she can shake her head and say, "Eating those 'poison sundaes' again," and help him remember the long-term risks involved with smoking. (We do not actually recommend that you do this with your own child. The risks of putting real poison in food are too great. However, you might read this, as well as the other opening vignettes, to your kids as a basis for discussion.)

Why Kids Smoke

To understand teen smoking, we have to break the question about why teens smoke into two parts. First, why do they start smoking? And second, why do about a third of those who start go on to become regular smokers? We can answer the first question in a single word: *cool*. Kids who try smoking perceive it to be cool. This coolness may be derived from the sophisticated adults they have seen smoking in real life or in movies. It may come from a rebellious, slightly antisocial sense of coolness they have seen among peers who smoke. It may be a fun and exciting brand of coolness they picked up from advertising. Whatever the origin, you can be sure that if smoking were not deemed cool to kids, you'd have to threaten them to make them do it.

Recent research conducted by the National Institutes of Health suggests that the most powerful factor in determining whether or not a teen smokes is whether or not his friends smoke. Teens who have friends who smoke are nine times as likely to smoke as those who hang out with kids who don't smoke. What determines whether a group of friends smoke? It is usually the influence of one or two naturally cool trendsetters in the group. These are the extroverted, charismatic, attractive, devil-may-care kids who seem to be natural leaders among teenagers. Think about your own teen days, and you can probably remember some of these extra-cool kids who others wanted to imitate.

Now let's consider the second question. Why do a third of the teens who try smoking become regular users? Conversely, why do two-thirds either remain occasional users or quit the habit altogether? The answer to this seems to be related to the addictive nature of nicotine and how it affects different people. A study at the

University of Michigan found that almost everyone who tries cigarettes does not like the taste the first time. However, what seems to separate those that become heavy smokers is the "buzz" or pleasant "high" that they got from the experience. Of those who experimented a few times and never smoked again, only about 25 percent of them got any kind of high from the experience. Of those who smoked for a while, then quit, about half recalled their first experience well. But of the heavy users, 78 percent remembered getting a good buzz from their first puffs. Apparently, some people have brain chemistry that makes them more easily hooked on nicotine than others.

Is there any way to tell which people are more likely to have this brain chemistry and therefore be more at risk to addiction? As it turns out, there may be. Do you remember those *cool* kids who become trendsetters that we talked about earlier? These kids who are extroverted, rebellious, sexually precocious, bluntly honest, impulsive, social, sensation seekers also fit the profile of the typical heavy smoker. They are cool *and* they are more easily addicted to nicotine. Because other kids want to be cool like them, they try smoking, too. Depending on their own genetic makeup, this copycat behavior leads to heavy smoking with some of them, but does not with the majority.

There is one other area of research that is important for you to know about. Research has linked smoking to depression. At first glance you might think that perhaps smoking causes depression in some people. But actually, the reverse seems to be true. Nicotine works in the brain to boost the production of two key neurotransmitters: dopamine and norepinephrine. These go to the pleasure center of the brain, the prefrontal cortex, and act to create a sense of well-being, temporarily treating the depression. This explains why there is a much higher incidence of smoking in psychiatric patients in general and even among twelve-to fifteen-year-olds with emotional and behavioral problems in particular. The good news is that certain antidepressant drugs have been shown to be of significant help in getting people to quit smoking. Such drugs seem to act on the brain in similar ways to nicotine without the health risks. Finding medications and psychotherapeutic methods of helping children and teens deal with depression should also make them less at risk for using tobacco to medicate themselves.

Finally, keep in mind that almost 90 percent of smokers began before the age of eighteen. In fact, some begin as early as age eight, with the middle school years of twelve to fourteen being the prime time for many to experiment and to begin getting hooked. It seems to take about three years to build up a full addiction to nicotine. Therefore, the teen years provide a critical opportunity for parents to prevent any experimentation with tobacco or to intercede in the addiction process before it becomes full blown.

What Kids Need to Know

Parents are never going to seem as cool to their kids as the cool kids do. Even so, what we tell our kids about smoking can make an important difference. The same NIH study that found that the smoking behavior of a teen's friends was the best predictor of whether or not a teen will start smoking also found that teens who said that their parents would be upset if they were caught smoking were much less likely to smoke. What we as parents say and do can clearly make a difference in our kids' choices on this critical matter.

If your kids do not ask you about tobacco, then look for a good opportunity to initiate a discussion yourself. When possible, find a good bridge to the subject. For example, if you are watching a movie or TV show together where one of the characters smokes, wait until after the show, then ask, "What did you think about that guy who always had a cigarette dangling from his mouth?" If you see some teens smoking in the parking lot, ask your child what she thinks about teen smoking. When you are out to eat together and you ask to sit in the No Smoking section of a restaurant, you've got a good ten minutes before the food comes to talk about why you made that choice.

Remembering our three-step approach to talking with kids, begin by asking good questions. Then listen to the answers *actively* and with *empathy*. Do not become judgmental or critical of their ideas, but look for common ground where you can agree. Also, because kids are being offered cigarettes at younger and younger ages, you can have this talk as early as age eight. Just keep your words and ideas at a level that they can understand. With younger kids, it is enough to disparage smoking where you see it. For example, saying "yuck" or "stinky" in front of your child when you see someone smoking on TV is a simple and nonobtrusive way of letting her know that you don't approve of smoking.

STEP 1. ASK GOOD QUESTIONS

Here are some examples of questions you can use to begin a discussion with older kids:

- Why do you think that I chose to sit in the No Smoking section?

- What do you think when you see teens smoking?

- What have they taught you in school about smoking?

- What are some reasons you would give your own teenager for not smoking?

■ Why do you think some teenagers smoke even though it is so dangerous?

STEP 2. BE PERSUASIVE

Being careful not to lecture, let you kids know how bad you would feel if they became smokers and to give some good concrete reasons for wanting them to abstain. Be sure that you talk from the place in your heart that loves them and cares about their health and happiness. If they ever feel that you are just trying to run their lives or look good yourself, there is a good chance that your words will backfire, hooking their rebellious side and making smoking more appealing. Any of the following arguments can help you build a strong case against smoking. But use your knowledge of your child to know which ones are likely to have the desired effect.

The Health Risks

Although many kids are not motivated by what may or may not happen in thirty years, it is still useful for them to know about the risks to their health that smoking can cause. Keep in mind that the more graphic that you can make your argument, the more emotionally powerful it will be. In fact, the Canadian government has now required that one side of cigarette cartons be used to graphically display the risks of smoking. Instead of a simple written message that "tobacco has been shown to cause cancer," they show a large picture of a cancer-ridden lung. They have done the same with other diseases, such as heart disease (a picture of a diseased heart) and gum disease (with a large picture of the most disgusting mouth you've ever seen). Talk about a profound "yuck" experience. Why are they doing this? Because they found that graphics were 60 times more effective than words alone. It appears that a picture *is* worth a thousand words, so find photos, videos, or anything else that will give your health message some "yuck" effect.

You can also increase the impact of the message by having it delivered by a victim of a tobacco-related disease. If you have a friend or a relative who has suffered such an illness, arrange a meeting with your teenager (this is a PG-13 experience, not for children). Is the person still in the hospital? That's even better. Don't be afraid of intruding on this person. Chances are the patient will appreciate the opportunity to use his mistake to help someone else avoid the torture he is going through, or dying from.

If your child is into sports, be sure to point out that professional athletes don't smoke, because it causes shortness of breath, puts added strain on the heart, can wreck lungs, and reduce the oxygen available for muscles used during sports, reducing performance and endurance.

The Short-Term Risks . . . Especially the "Yuck" Effect

Remember, kids first try smoking when they think it's cool. This is why most of the advertising campaigns try to make smoking look either cool or disgusting, depending on the goals for the campaign. Whatever information you can give your kids to turn *cool* into *yuck* will help build their resistance to trying cigarettes or quitting them. The following information should help:

■ Smoking causes bad breath, yellows teeth, and increases the risk of gum disease, even tooth loss. No wonder in one study,

78 percent of teenage boys said they do not like kissing girls who smoke.

- Smoking makes your hair stink, your clothes stink, your car stink, and your house stink.

- Smoking dulls your taste buds and sense of smell so that food doesn't taste as good.

- Spit tobacco can cause cracked lips, white spots, sores, bleeding in the mouth, and oral cancer.

- Smoking can cause chronic coughing, increased phlegm, wheezing, and make you look like your great-grandmother on a bad day.

- In other words, smoking will not only wreck your health, but your looks, too.

It's Cool Not to Smoke

We recently asked a couple of teens why they and their friends did not smoke. Their answer? "It's not considered cool in our group." This attitude is a parent's dream come true. If the result of massive media campaigns, education, and parent conversations can help make smoking not cool, then we will continue to see dramatic reductions in teen smoking rates. You can help by exposing your child to these campaigns. If you see an ad in a magazine that makes smoking look disgusting, cut it out and give it to your teen. Talk to her about the message of the ad, without lecturing. If you are watching TV together and a smoking-prevention commercial comes on, take time to talk about it later. Finally, many cool teen celebrities are helping by developing antismoking websites. Help your child find these sites and look at them together. Remember, kids want to be like the kids they think are cool. So, if the cool kids think smoking is stupid, it's a positive influence.

STEP 3. TALK ABOUT THE CONSEQUENCES

After talking with your teen about all the good reasons not to use tobacco in any form, even those cute little *bidis* (tiny, flavored cigarettes from India or Southeast Asia) or *kreteks* (clove cigarettes from Indonesia) that are rapidly gaining in popularity, it is important for you to let your kids know that it is not all right for them to use tobacco. Try to get an agreement that they will not smoke and even put it in writing.

The last section talked about the *natural* consequences of smoking. In other words, those consequences provided by Mother Nature. Unfortunately, many of the most serious of these do not occur for a long time. You can reduce this time lag, and the tendency for kids to ignore consequences that happen much later, by adding a layer of *logical* consequences. These are consequences that you as a parent enforce to show kids what logically follows when they break family rules or the needs of the situation. Remember from chapter 2, we are not trying to use so much force that the logical consequences become *the* reason that your teen does not smoke. We want him to decide that he is not smoking for his own good, so that years later when you aren't around to ground him, he will still avoid smoking. The logical consequences are just an added reason and one that lets your teen know how serious you are about this issue. Therefore, do not become heavy-handed or too punitive. Some good logical consequences for smoking might include:

- Loss of freedom. If your teen smokes, then it is logical that you keep a closer eye on him. This means staying home more often and missing some parties or other social events until you feel that he can keep his word again.

- Loss of the use of the car. This follows logically from loss of freedom.

- Loss of privacy. If your teen smokes, you may want to begin searching her backpack and room for a period of time to make sure she isn't hiding cigarettes. (We do not recommend such search tactics with kids who are behaving responsibly and cooperatively, as it will be seen as an unjust invasion of privacy and potentially damage the trust that you have built together over many years.)

- A visit to the family physician. If your teen is smoking, he may need help in quitting, depending on how long he has been using and his level of addiction. A doctor can help recommend a course of treatment that might include counseling, patches or other aids, and even antidepressant medication.

Practice Peer-Pressure Refusal Lines

Let's say that you have talked with your child about not smoking. You have asked good questions, listened respectfully, made persuasive arguments (including graphics, metaphors, testimonies, and other resources), and added logical consequences. Let's also say that your teen agrees with you 100 percent that smoking is like eating a poison sundae and only an idiot would do that. So, you are home free, right? Of course not. Don't ever think you are home free. Kids change their minds all the time, sometimes 180 degrees. And what often creates the change is peer pressure.

Peer pressure is not usually the in-your-face teasing and challenging ("Come on, don't be such a baby!") that we usually think it is. Instead, it's five friends sitting around talking when one pulls out a package of cigarettes and lights up. He passes it to the next and then the next. By the time it reaches the fifth person, there is an enormous unspoken pressure to go along with the group. It takes awareness, courage, and skill to resist. This is where parents can help. First, talk with your kids about peer pressure and how subtle a force it can be. Predict that they will be tempted to go along with the crowd many times in their lives, and that they need to think about when this is useful and when it is a bad decision. Ask them what they can say when offered cigarettes so that they will not feel foolish doing so. This is critical, because they want to avoid feeling foolish almost at all costs. Helping them come up with clever refusal lines can give them the confidence and skill to say no when the time comes. Go over some of these suggestions together, helping decide what style of refusal feels best to them. Then let them practice role-playing their lines while you play a teenager trying to get him to join you for a smoke.

Ways to Say No to Peer Pressure Without Feeling Foolish

- **Use humor:**
  - "No, thanks. I like my teeth to be white, not yellow."

  - "No, thanks. That cigarette doesn't go with my outfit."

  - "No, thanks. My boyfriend doesn't like kissing an ashtray."

- **Reverse the Pressure:**
  - "Is this what you do to be cool?"
  - "I bet you can't go a week with smoking."

- **Ask a Question:**
  - "Now, why would I want to do something that smells that bad?"
  - "Do you know any professional athletes who smoke?"
  - "Why would I want to do that to my lungs?"

- **Change the Subject:**
  - "No, thanks. Hey, have you seen any great movies lately?"

- **Be Direct:**
  - "To tell you the truth, I'm not into that."
  - "I'd rather spend my money on other stuff."
  - "No, thanks. I like being healthy."

QUESTIONS KIDS SOMETIMES ASK (AND POSSIBLE ANSWERS)

Q. *If smoking is so bad for you, why do you smoke?*

This is a tough question because it speaks directly to your credibility. Your best answer, of course, is something like the following:

A.1. You're right. I'll make a deal with you. I'll quit if you promise never to start.

This is a powerful offer, but you have to follow through or your credibility is damaged. If you aren't ready to make this offer, then use your own experience as a negative example, like this:

A.2. The sneaky thing about smoking is this: When you start, you think that you can quit anytime you want. But I can tell you from my own experience that it's a very hard habit to give up. In fact, it is a whole lot easier never to start smoking than it is to give it up. That's why I want you never to even try it.

Q. *Why are you making such a big deal out of this? It's not like I'm doing drugs or something.*

A. Tobacco can be just as lethal as anything out there. In fact, an estimated four million teenagers will eventually die from tobacco-related illnesses like cancer, heart disease, and lung disease. I'm making a big deal out of this because I love you and don't want you to be one of them.

Q. *Why are you always trying to run my life?!*

Turn your palms up, a gesture indicating peace and lack of control, and say in a gentle voice:

A. Listen, I don't know what decision you will make when you are an adult. And my job as your parent is not to run your life. It is my job, however, to help you stay safe and healthy while you are learning what you really want for yourself. Smoking is just one of those things that is far too dangerous for me to stand back and let you learn the hard way. I love you and don't want to see you hurt.

Work to Prevent Teen Smoking in Your Community

There has been a tremendous effort by numerous groups in recent years to lower the teen smoking rate. Parents, educators, health professionals, the government, and even some tobacco companies are putting tremendous money and effort into this important goal. Look for ways to help in your own community. And if you really want to help your teen do some good, as well as solidify her own decision not to smoke, take her with you. We have made a good deal of headway in handling this challenge, and with the active support of concerned parents, we can help many other teens learn to recognize a poison sundae when they see it.

A Brief Review

With three thousand children and teens trying their first cigarette each day, it is imperative that parents talk with their children soon and often about living smoke-free lives. Getting through about the risks of smoking requires asking good questions, making persuasive arguments, and talking about the consequences. Be sure to go beyond the health risks of smoking to include the short-term risks such as yellow teeth, bad breath, and "yucky" kissing. Since most kids smoke when they see it as cool, teaching kids how to resist peer pressure without looking foolish is also a valuable skill. Finally, if you smoke, consider quitting. If you are not ready to quit, use your own experience as testimony to just how addictive tobacco can be.

Chapter 14

Violence and Safety

It had gotten so he dreaded the bus ride home. He could avoid him at school, but there was nowhere to hide on the bus. It wasn't his fault that he was late developing and still small for thirteen, but he knew that it made him an easy target for kids like Jonathon. How many times would he hand over his lunch money and take the slaps and taunting? Maybe Jonathon was right and he was nothing but a loser. He certainly felt like one. He didn't have any real friends, and his parents were too busy fighting to notice that he was in trouble. They didn't even seem to mind that his grades had fallen steadily over the past year—the year of the Beast, as he called it, his private name for Jonathon, the oversize fourteen-year-old that had made his life so miserable this year.

What to do, what to do? Maybe he should stand up to Jonathon and fight it out like a man. He'd read about a kid trying that. This kid had challenged *his* personal beast to a fistfight after they got off the bus, only the beast hit him in the back of the head as he walked down the stairs from the bus and broke an artery or something, and the kid died. Unhappy ending. No, thanks. Maybe he should pull a Columbine and borrow one of Dad's guns. He'd walk right up to Jonathon in the middle of the lunchroom and say, "Now who's the loser?" then blow him away. He'd probably spend a lot of time in prison for that, but at least he'd have his revenge. Besides, he might get his picture in *Time* magazine like that wimpy-looking kid who took out two students in California that time. One thing for sure, he couldn't live like *this* much longer. Something was about to blow inside his head. He could feel it. Say, maybe he could be as bad as Jonathon. Maybe.

What Parents Need to Know

All caring parents worry about their children's safety. We understand the fragility of life and how tragedy can strike in an instant. We warn our kids not to open the door to strangers, and then wonder why they forget and still do. We stare at the television in disbelief every time a school shooting or terrorist attack takes a life. We want to trust people, but we are sometimes wary. We know the horror stories, and we are sometimes afraid.

The history of the human race gives cause for optimism *and* concern. From the time we first shared caves with prehistoric beasts, we have recognized that, like it or not, we were engaged in a battle of survival of the fittest, and that a club and a smile usually won out over just a smile. Our history is replete with examples of assault, murder, domestic violence, child abuse, rape, war and terrorism. Bullies like Jonathon may strike terror in the hearts of their schoolmate victims, but they pale in comparison with the historical acts of tyrants throughout history. Progress in the march from violence to peace has come through the rule of law and the pursuit of justice, but it has come gradually, moving up and down like the stock market.

Teaching our children how to survive in an often-violent world while simultaneously teaching them to be peacemakers is a daunting task. But not to teach these important lessons is to let our children, and our society, flounder on the shoals between victim and abuser. Victims have always had a tendency to identify with the aggressor and unconsciously seek to be like their tormentors. In today's world of school shootings, workplace violence, and terrorism, these victims (as well as those who simply perceive themselves as victims) are striking back with alarming frequency. What can parents do to get through to their children about solving conflicts nonviolently while still taking necessary steps to secure their safety? How do we help them, especially our sons, tame the savage beast that lives in the dark reaches of their own mind so that anger, violence, and revenge do not rule in place of law, order, and forgiveness? And how do we do it without paralyzing them with fear or stifling the natural need to defend oneself against aggression?

We begin by opening the channels of communication with our kids at an early age. Talking with them often about events in their lives with an understanding and empathetic ear helps give them the courage to talk to us later when issues of violence and safety arise. We continue by emphasizing such values as justice, nonviolent conflict resolution, forgiveness, cooperation, safety, and self-defense. We teach them skills for problem solving, negotiation, and getting help. If need be, we also get them karate lessons. With this as the framework, we are ready to build on the specifics of helping them reduce their own violent tendencies while staying safe in a world where others sometimes give free rein to their own. The following tips provide information in areas that you will want to address:

Tips for Raising Safe Yet Nonviolent Children in a Violent World

1. **Talk about safety.** Some kids have a natural cautiousness about them while others blindly rush in where angels fear to tread. Watch for your child's tendencies, knowing that with more adventurous children you will have to do more talking and be eternally vigilant. However, even with cautious children, they do not have the experience to know where danger may be lurking or how to handle it once confronted. The challenge is to teach your children to be reasonably cautious without scaring them into an unhealthy fear of people or new places. Also know that for most kids, *fun* is high up on their list of values while *safety* is not. We have to constantly reinforce the idea that fun is only okay when it happens safely.

   With young children (those under the age of five) talk about the rules of a situation and the need to be safe. For example, in a shopping mall, you might say the following: "It is very important that you stay with me all the time when we are away from home so that nothing bad happens to you and you don't get lost." You do not want to scare them by going into details about kidnapping, but you do want to remind them often that they are never to go with strangers. However, do not be lulled into thinking that a young child is ever safe without a responsible adult watching them. Young children are no match for child predators, no matter how well the child has been coached.

   As kids get older they will want reasons behind your rules. Parents who rely on the old "because I'm the parent and I said so" not only invite rebellion but also miss a great opportunity to get through. Let them know that there are some people, not many, but some, who might kidnap or hurt children left alone. Some kids may resist your conversations about kidnapping or other dangers, afraid to even think about the possibility. Be gentle and do not overwhelm them, but let them know that there are risks and that is why you have certain rules for their safety. For example: "The reason you are never to go to the rest room alone is that there are some people, fortunately very few people, but still some people who look for chances to harm children. You are much safer if someone is with you."

When kids are old enough to be in public without adult supervision, it is important to talk about lures that child predators use to get kids alone. Make sure they know never to go with strangers, no matter what the stranger says or how nice he or she seems. Brainstorm with your kids to think of lures that these predators might use. For example: "Your mother was in an accident and your dad's at the hospital. I'm a social worker there and I'm here to take you to see them." Or "We're shooting a music video in the parking lot and need a couple of extras. I think you would be perfect, and who knows, it might start a career."

With teenagers, who are often without adult supervision, play "what if." Think of situations in which they could be in danger and ask them what they would do. Then discuss the possible consequences or their actions and brainstorm other options. For example, "What if you were at a fast-food place and another teenager came up to you and accused you of cutting him off in the parking lot. You could tell he was looking for a fight. What would you do to avoid one?"

2. **Make and enforce rules for nonviolence and safety.** We suggest that families have a "no hitting" rule. This means that prob-

lems must be resolved by nonviolent means. Even a toddler can be taught "people are not for hitting." Give him a choice to either play without hitting (or biting or scratching) or to go to a time-out area until he is ready to play without hitting. If he continues to hit, remove him for five minutes the first time. Then give him a choice to try again: "Do you think you are ready to play without hitting?" If he agrees, bring him back to be with the others. If he hits again, tell him, "I see you need some time alone again," or "It's okay to be angry, but not to hit people. Let's go back to time-out for a little longer this time." Let him stay about ten minutes this time before trying again.

It is obviously counterproductive to spank kids for being violent. While your verbal message is that hitting is not an okay way to handle problems, the nonverbal message that comes through the spanking is just the opposite. In fact, spanking in general carries this message and is better left out of the discipline arsenal. There are many more effective methods available and plenty of good books and even courses that are available for teaching you how to manage behavior without this technique.

As parents we want to be always aware of the safety risks involved in any activity. Although it is fine for kids to learn many of life's lessons the hard way through the natural consequences of their actions, when the consequences can be catastrophic, we need rules and consequences to help our kids learn. For example, it is fine for a ten-year-old to learn how to ride a bike by falling off a number of times. The bumps and bruises that go with it are the proud badges of childhood. However, it is not okay for him to ride on busy streets or without a helmet, because the consequences are life-threatening.

Talk with your kids about the risks, and then, with their input, make rules to govern the situation. For example: "Always wear a helmet when riding; only ride in the cul-de-sac or driveway." Although kids should be encouraged to help make the rules, the parent has the final authority to make sure that the rules are reasonable. Violations of safety rules should result in loss of a logically connected privilege. For example, loss of the bike for a period of time is a good logical consequence for breaking a bike rule.

3. **Get your head out of the media sand and do something.** Our experience is that most parents need a wake-up call about the media messages that are helping to shape their kids' values. True, a violent movie or video game is not going to turn a well-adjusted teenager into a mass murderer. However, the research on the subject is overwhelming that violent media does have a negative impact in at least four ways: 1. It increases violent behavior. 2. It can lead to copycat violence, particularly with kids who are already very hurt, angry, and discouraged. 3. It can create extreme fear in children. 4. It causes desensitization. This last effect is perhaps the most insidious. John Michael Murray in his documentary video, *Think About It: The Impact of Media Violence*, uses the following example to demonstrate how all of us have become somewhat desensitized to violence through sheer repetition: Imagine a beautiful golden retriever on a movie screen. Now imagine him being shot to death by automatic weapon fire. How does it make you feel? Probably a little sick. Yet we can watch thirty-three humans killed the same way in a movie like *Die Hard II* without much reaction. Why? We have seen so much of this kind of violence that we have become desensitized to it. The golden

retriever scene is still new, and it still moves us. Talk with your kids about why seeing too much violence and experiencing it through graphic video games or hearing it through music lyrics is not good for them. Although it is unlikely that your words will get through entirely, you will at least set the stage for limiting their behavior. For example, let them know that PG-13 means that they will need to be thirteen before they can see go such a movie. The same is true with video games. Use the rating codes and then check out the games for yourself to make sure that it does not show excessively graphic violence, denigrate women, or otherwise violate your family values.

Along these lines, it is important to take the time to experience your kids' media with them so you will know what messages are coming through. Watch some of their programs with them on TV, play some of their video and computer games together, and listen to their music. During times of crisis even watch the news together. Talk about the messages that come through the experience, especially those that relate to your values. Talk with them about the effects of too much violence, and suggest to them that what they are really wanting is adventure, and not necessarily violence. Help them find shows and games that satisfy the teen/ preteen craving for adventure in ways that are not excessively violent. You can also use the stories you watch together on TV or video to ask them how they would handle situations that come up in the shows. Talk about both the mistakes that characters made, as well as the positive choices. Because of the emotional experience of such stories, your kids will be tuned in and more available for you to get through to with positive messages of your own. Also invite them to watch the news or other informative shows with you and discuss real-world violence and its consequences. Help them understand the seriousness of real-life violence and why it is too important to be trivialized in games and movies.

We also recommend that you keep computers and video games in a public part of the house so that you can see what is going on. This also helps break up the isolating aspects of kids holing up in their rooms for hours upon hours. Along these lines, be sure to limit the amount of entertainment *screen time* that your children are allowed on school days and then on weekends and holidays. While some studies have shown that kids spend as much as an average of 6.5 hours a day of *screen time* with media, we recommend limiting this to no more than an hour a school day of entertainment media and no more than three hours a day on weekends and holidays.

4. **Pay special attention to the Internet.** The Internet offers a special area of risk for children and teens. It is a wide-open window to the world, and much of what flies in through that window is appalling. Along with the educational opportunities that make it too great a gift to throw out with the bathwater, the Internet also offers unrestrained access to erotica; violent Web sites such as the Nazi site that was a favorite of Eric Harris and Dylan Kleibold, the Columbine shooters; consumer pitches of all kinds including outright scams; and a hunting ground for child abusers and sexual predators to lure kids into real-life relationships. It is imperative that you talk with your kids about these risks, sharing any true "horror stories" that you can find to make it real to them. Then together, make a list of rules governing their use of the Internet. These should include the parental controls and filters offered by Internet carriers that allow you to limit what sites your children can

view. You should also know how to check the history file on the computer to see what sites have been visited during the past three weeks. We also think that live chat should only be allowed in approved chat rooms, and that kids never give out their full name, phone number, or address without parental permission. The computer should be in a public area, and parents need the right to look over their kids' shoulder from time to time to make sure they are following the rules. If this sounds harsh, keep in mind that the Internet is a seductive, perhaps even addictive, tool that can easily get out of control. It is also the likely future of education and information, and kids who do not learn to use it effectively will likely lag behind. So it is worth the trouble to do it safely.

5. **Talk with other parents.** Parenting against the norm is very difficult. What parent hasn't heard the plaintiff refrain "But all the other kids' parents let them!" Fortunately, as Napoleon once observed about human nature, "People don't want liberty; they want equality." In other words, your kids don't really want to do what they want to do as much as they do not want to be the only kids not allowed to do it. For example, nobody complains about not being able to get a driver's license at fifteen because nobody else can get one, either. That's equality. Being a ten-year-old who is not allowed to watch PG-13 movies would not be so bad either if all the other kids were not allowed to watch them. The more parents in a community can band together to discuss reasonable rules for safety and violence prevention, the easier it is for all parents to enforce them.

6. **Talk about terrorism and war.** The 21st century has brought a particularly atrocious form of war to the forefront of civiliza-

tion: terrorism. It is important to explain this to children in language appropriate for their age. Even young children can understand that terrorists are very angry people who try to get what they want by attacking people and places. When people hurt other people they have to be stopped. Sometimes this means going to war against these people. Wars that are meant to stop people from hurting other people are just wars, and our country has to fight such wars from time to time.

During times of war and/or terrorism, it is important to reassure your children as much as is possible that we have the strength and the ability to protect them from harm. If this requires their cooperation in some way, then tell them what they must do to help. In fact, where a real threat exists to the child, involving her in some helpful action can help reduce anxiety. It is also useful to keep as normal a routine as possible and to focus on the positives that can come out of such a challenging situation. Acts of heroism, patriotism, and leadership can provide lessons that are invaluable. Take time to talk about your other values such as faith beliefs, courage and justice. For example, during the attacks on America by Muslim extremists, it is important to talk to kids about the injustice of stereotyping all Muslims or Arabs as bad when it is only a small percentage of such people who have wronged us.

QUESTIONS KIDS SOMETIMES ASK (AND POSSIBLE ANSWERS)

Questions related to safety and violence are often unasked due to embarrassment or fear of reprisal from a bully. The young teenager in the opening vignette would have been unlikely to ask his parents for advice concerning his bully due to his poor relationship with them. Being nonjudgmental, empathetic, and encouraging when you talk with children about their problems from an early age on can help make you an askable parent in times of genuine trouble. Even so, there are times when all parents must pick up on the nonverbal cues that tell us that something is wrong with our child. We need to listen to the unasked questions that lie beneath their benign inquiries. For example:

Q. *When you were little did anyone ever pick of you?*

Your parental warning light should be flashing with a question like this. It is unlikely that the child has suddenly developed an interest in parental history. What is more likely is that he has a similar problem and is looking for clues about how to handle it. Answer the question, but then respond to the child's feelings in a way that lets him know you are on his side, and probe for problems.

A. Hmm. I guess most kids have run into a bully at one time or another. When I was about five this older kid scared me real bad by telling me that an Indian totem pole came alive at night and that if I told anyone about it, it would get me. So, I was afraid to tell my parents, who could have let me know that what he said wasn't true. It was a pretty mean thing for him to have done.

Q. *What did you do?*

A. Well, I guess I moped around being scared until my parents noticed that something was wrong and asked me about it. I told them I couldn't tell, but they said that it was always right to tell your parents, so I did. I'm really glad that I did, because they let me know that totem poles can't hurt you. Bullys can be really scary, and it's hard to know what to do sometimes. Have you run into a bully?

Q. *Are the terrorists going to attack us too?*

Anytime that there is a major violent event in the news, many kids will become fearful that something similar will happen to them. In fact the more similar the event is to their situation and the closer to home, the more concerned they will be. While you want to reassure them that they are safe, you also want to take the opportunity to use the emotionally-charged issue to help reinforce sound beliefs, attitudes, and values.

A. That was an awful tragedy. It hurt a lot of people and a lot more were scared. We cannot be completely sure that it will never happen here, but the chances are that we are safe. For one thing, we live in a very strong country and our leaders are taking the right steps to make sure that the people who did this terrible thing are caught and that others are prevented from doing anything else like it. For another thing, it's a very large country so the chances of them attacking us here are pretty small. Still, it takes courage to face this challenge. Do you know what courage is? It's the feeling that says even though we may be afraid, we will keep going and doing what must be done—like going to school and to work and to play. Terrorists try to make us afraid to do those things, but we won't let them stop us. We have too much courage for that. Now, let's talk about what we can do for the victims of this tragedy. Some people are writing letters of sympathy to their families; others are collecting money to help their families. What are some things we might do to let them know that we care about them and that we are all in this together?

Q. *Why did Clark commit suicide?*

The suicide of a schoolmate or someone in a child's or teen's immediate community is always cause for concern, not just for the victim, but for other discouraged kids who take a twisted sort of courage from the act and become copycat suicides. Parents of teens and even preteens who are experiencing a lot of stress and seem depressed or anxious should be particularly guarded, because suicides often occur in clusters. It is important to talk with kids about suicide when this happens, whether they ask or not. The goal is to persuade the child that suicide is always a bad choice for kids, while being careful not to put down the victim himself.

A. I don't know why Clark made such a bad decision. Psychologists say that there are different reasons people sometimes take their own life. Some just are so discouraged with the way things are going that they want to get it over with. This is pretty foolish when you think about it, because things can always get better if you stay alive, but they can never get better if you're dead. Other people commit suicide as a way of getting even with someone they think has hurt them. Like when a girl breaks up with a guy and he shoots himself. This is supposed to make the girl feel bad. And maybe it does . . . for a little while. But she eventually gets over it, and he's still dead. So, again, not very smart. Plus, in our family we believe that it is wrong to kill anybody, unless it's in self-defense, even yourself. Life is too precious to waste. (Other questions you can ask to keep the discussion going: Why do you think he did it? What other, better choices did he have? Where can someone get help when he feels so bad he thinks about suicide?)

Q. *Why was the Garretts' house destroyed in the tornado? Were they bad?*

Young children will sometimes believe that mysterious events like tornados are punishments for having been bad. Gently correct them and explain that nature—or God, if you prefer—has a way of operating that we do not always understand.

A. No, the Garretts were not being punished for being bad. Nature doesn't work like that. Sometimes bad things happen to good people. We don't always understand why, but we try to help each other through the hard times. Maybe that's a positive way at looking at these things. The strong communities pull together to get through them, and it makes them better for it. The selfish ones just try to take care of themselves, and they grow weaker. What do you think that we can do to help the Garretts?

Q. *Why do some people hurt children?*

If this question follows a news story about a child who was hurt, then stick to the question. However, if there has been no recent story on the news or in your community, explore for the possibility that your child is afraid of someone she knows hurting her or having hurt her. Make sure that you remain calm, though concerned, no matter what the answers may be, because your anxiety or panic will make the situation much worse. If you do uncover a problem or possible problem, you will want to contact the proper authorities. For example, the police department's Crimes Against Children division or the Department of Child and Family Services.

A. People who hurt children have some very serious problems, and they have to be stopped. No one should ever hurt a child. If they do, then the child should tell another adult even if she is afraid. Then the adult can call the police and make sure that person can't hurt the child anymore. Do you know someone who has hurt a child? Has an adult ever hurt you? Has anyone scared you?

Q. *Is it okay to fight back if I'm picked on?*

This is a question for our changing times. When we were growing up, the answer, at least for boys, was that it was not only okay, but expected that you would fight back if picked on or teased beyond reasonable limits. In fact, one of the surest ways of provoking a fight was to insult the other kid's family, particularly his mother. Schools are increasingly sensitive to the escalation of fighting that can lead from pushing and shoving to hitting to weapons. These days schools are more often clamping down on both parties for fighting and showing little tolerance for violence. Find out your school's policy, but the following answer is probably good advice regardless.

A. This is a tough question. You are always better off avoiding a fight. For one thing, you never know if the other guy is going to fight fair or fight dirty. Sometimes kids who would normally fight fair get so mad, they pick up something and hit you with it. This can be really dangerous. Older kids, these days, sometimes come back with guns or knives. You should never let someone goad you into a fight. It may take courage to walk away from someone calling you names or insulting your family, but you have to do it. The only exception is if you are attacked and there is no way out but to fight—like when America was attacked by terrorists. (Follow-up questions might include: What does your school tell you to do if someone is picking on you? Has someone been picking on you? What ways of handling it have you seen or thought of that might work? How can you use words to defuse a charged situation instead of provoking violence?)

A Brief Review

Children are more vulnerable to acts of violence and issues of safety than adults, though they often do not have the knowledge or experience to know it. Getting through to them is a matter of talking often about safety risks and other dangers, while being careful not to paralyze them with fear. Make and enforce safety rules from an early age, and take time to discuss news events from your community and the world at large as a platform for discussing your values concerning violence and its prevention. Be especially aware of signs that your child is being picked on or is otherwise afraid. Then become an ally in helping him decides how to handle the situation, or when necessary, intervene yourself.

Conclusion

There is a scene in the movie *Pearl Harbor* in which sailors trapped in the hull of a sinking battleship bang on the metal for help as rescuers frantically attempt to cut through with a blowtorch to save them from drowning. As the precious moments tick by, we see the hands of two trapped sailors reaching in desperation through a crack in the ship. Even so, the grim reality sets in that they are not going to make it. As their hands go limp, the camera pans back to show the mournful workers on deck, the sinking warship and finally, the smoking devastation of the entire harbor.

Everyone tells parents how important it is to talk with their children about the critical issues of our times. But as the saying goes, talk is cheap. And communication is not enough. The sailors working to free their trapped comrades in the torpedoed ship were able to communicate. What they were unable to do was get through the thick metal in time to make a difference.

A superficial overview of this book may give parents the idea that this is just another book about the importance of talking to children about some of the critical issues of our times. It is not. The point of this book is that we as parents must do more than just talk with our kids. We must develop the persuasive ability to *get through*. We must become powerful blowtorches that cut through the metal of their indifference and free their endangered minds.

We have demonstrated throughout this book that we do this by engaging them in dialogue, not by indulging ourselves in lecture. We learn to ask good questions and to provide compelling answers to their questions. We use discipline when necessary, but understand that discipline alone is never enough to win over a mind. We focus not just on the facts, but also on the values that make the facts important. We use repetition, and we repeat ourselves using a variety of learning modalities. We don't just talk. We teach through example, through letters and E-mail, by discussing real-life experiences when they happen, by creating memorable metaphors and sharing poignant stories, by encouraging our children's positive words and actions, and through other creative methods that we discover will get through to one child, if not another.

To help you know whether or not you are getting through to your child, we suggest that you wait two or three weeks following a talk and then ask the following: "If you were the parent and I were the child/teen what would you want me to know about _____?" Follow this up by asking: "If you were the parent and I were the child/teen how would you convince me that_____?" Their answers should give you an idea about how well your views on a given topic have gotten through and stuck. Of course, kids will sometimes tell us what they think we want to hear whether it is what they truly believe or not. Therefore, the only sure way to know if you have gotten through is to watch their walk, not just listen to their talk. When people say one thing, but do another, trust that their behavior reveals their attitude and not their words. When this happens, rather than get upset, recognize that you will need to find new ways to get through, and try again.

One of the goals for this book is to help you prevent major problems from occurring in your family. However, there are times when the problems that some children have are more severe than parents can handle alone. In spite of our best efforts, kids will sometimes make bad decisions. They may knuckle under to peer pressure or yield to the stresses of their hectic lives. Some may have chemical imbalances caused by nature. Whatever the cause, the results can be devastating for a family—anything from drug addiction, pregnancy, and other behavioral problems to full-blown mental health issues. When such challenges occur, wise parents will use whatever strength they can muster to remain calm under fire. They know that their kids are trapped under the hull of a sinking ship, with time of the essence. They do not waste this time playing the blame game. Their energy is too precious to be consumed in guilt. Perhaps most important, they are not too proud to get help. They use whatever professionals they need to help them rescue their kids from the grasp of whatever it is that controls them.

Getting professional help when you can't get through is crucial. When you recognize that you do not have all the answers, this is a powerful answer in itself. Having the courage, love and will to do all you can to reclaim your kids is what matters most. And doing all that you can do is all that any of us can do.

We encourage you to make the time to address each of the topics in this book with your children as often and in as many ways as you think necessary to get through. When they resist your efforts, pull back for a time and approach from another direction later. Stay positive and loving as much as possible, letting them know that if you do not say the right thing every time it is not because you don't love them and want the best for them, but that you are human. Above all, speak from that place in your heart that cares more about their safety and happiness than you do about your own and you will be surprised many years later when you hear your own thoughts spoken from the mouths of your grandchildren and know for certain that you did *get through.*

Resources

Chapter 4: Alcohol and Other Drugs

BOOKS FOR TEENAGERS

Hyde, Margaret O., and John F. Setaro. *Alcohol 101: An Overview for Teens*. Colorado: Twenty First Century Books, 1999.

Folkers, Gladys, Jeanne Englemann, and Marie Olofsdotter. *Taking Charge of My Mind and Body: A Girl's Guide to Outsmarting Alcohol, Drugs, Smoking, and Eating Problems*. Minnesota: Free Spirit Publishing, 1997.

Kuhn, Cynthia, Scott Swartzwelder, and Wilkie Wilson. *Buzzed: The Straight Facts About the Most Used and Abused Drugs from Alcohol to Ecstasy*. 1998.

Rupp, Joseph C. *Drugs and Death: Profiles of Illegal Drug Abuse*. Texas: Deep 6 Productions, Inc., 1998.

Columbia University Health Education. *The Go Ask Alice Book of Answers: A Guide to Good Physical, Sexual, and Emotional Health*. New York: Owl Books, 1998.

BOOKS FOR PARENTS

Schwebel, Robert. *Saying No Is Not Enough: Helping Your Kids Make Wise Decisions About Alcohol, Tobacco, and Other Drugs*. New York: Newmarket Press, 1998.

Dupont, Jr., Robert L., M.D. *Getting Tough on Gateway Drugs—A Guide for the Family*. Washington. D.C.: American Psychiatric Press, 1984.

Rahrer, Stuart J. *Seven Sensible Strategies for Drug-Free Kids*. Washington, D.C.: Child Welfare League of America, 1999.

McMahon, Tom. *Teen Tips: A Practical Guide for Parents with Kids 11 to 19*. New York: Pocket Books, 1996.

ORGANIZATIONS AND WEB SITES

Alcoholics Anonymous (AA)
P.O. Box 459
Grand Central Station
New York, NY 10163
212/870-3400
Fax: 212/870-3003

Narcotics Anonymous (NA)
World Service Office
P.O. Box 9999
Van Nuys, CA 91409
818/773-9999
Fax: 818/700-0700
E-mail: *wso@aol.com*

The American Council for Drug Education
164 West 74th Street
New York, NY 10023
1-800-488-DRUG
Fax: 212/595-2553
www.acde.org

National Clearinghouse for Alcohol and Drug Information
P.O. Box 2345
Rockville, MD 20847-2345
1-800-729-6686
Fax: 301/468-6433
www.health.org

Drug Enforcement Administration
Demand Reduction Section, Office of Public Affairs
700 Army Navy Drive
Arlington, VA 22202
202/307-7936
Fax: 202/307-4559
www.dea.gov

National Council on Alcoholism and Drug Dependence, Inc.
20 Exchange Place, Suite 2902
New York, NY 10005
212/269-7797
Fax: 212/269-7510
Hopeline: 1-800-NCA-CALL
www.ncadd.org

Partnership for a Drug-Free America
405 Lexington Avenue, Suite 1601
New York, NY 10174
212/922-1560
Fax: 212/922-1570
www.drugfreeamerica.org

National Institute on Alcohol Abuse and Alcoholism (NIAAA)
Prevention Research Branch
Willco Building
6000 Executive Boulevard, Suite 505
Bethesda, MD 20892-7003
301/443-1677
Fax: 301/443-8774
www.niaaa.nih.gov/

National Institute on Drug Abuse
6001 Executive Boulevard, Room 5213
Bethesda, MD 20892
301/443-1124
www.drugabuse.gov/

Office of National Drug Control Policy
Executive Office of the President
Washington, DC 20503
www.whitehousedrugpolicy.gov/index.html

National Children's Coalition
www.child.net/drugalc.htm

Alcohol and Drug Services
5209 West Wendover Ave.
High Point, NC 27265
336/812-8645
Fax: 336/812-8656
www.adsyes.com/prevention.html

National Families in Action
Century Plaza II
2957 Clairmont Road, Suite 150
Atlanta, GA 30329
404/248-9676
Fax: 404/248-1312
www.nationalfamilies.org

Chapter 5: Courage and Fear
BOOKS FOR CHILDREN AGES 4–8

Tompert, Ann. *Will You Come Back for Me?* New York: Albert Whitman & Company, 1992.

Lobby, Theodore E. *Jessica and the Wolf: A Story for Children Who Have Bad Dreams*. New York: Magination Press, 1990.

Berenstain, Jan and Stan. *The Berenstain Bears in the Dark*. New York: Random House, 1982.

BOOKS FOR TEENAGERS

Waldman, Jackie. *Teens With the Courage to Give: Young People Who Triumphed over Tragedy and Volunteered to Make a Difference*. California: Conari Press, 2000.

BOOKS FOR PARENTS

Garber, Stephen W., Ph.D., Marianne Daniels Garber, and Robyn Freedman Spizman. *Monsters Under the Bed and Other Childhood Fears: Helping Your Child Overcome Anxieties, Fears, and Phobias*. New York: Villard Books, 1993.

Morris, Richard, and Thomas R. Kratochwill. *Treating Children's Fears and Phobias*. New York: Pergamon Press, 1983.

Schacter, Robert, and Carole Spearin McCauley. *When Your Child is Afraid*. New York: Simon & Schuster, 1988.

Ferber, Richard. *Solve Your Child's Sleep Problems*. New York: Fireside Books, 1985.

Ireland, Karin. *Boost Your Child's Self-Esteem: Simple, Effective Ways to Build Children's Self-Respect and Confidence*. New York: The Berkley Publishing Group, 2000.

Chapter 6: Death

BOOKS FOR CHILDREN AGES 4–8

Rylant, Cynthia. *Dog Heaven*. New York: Scholastic Trade, 1995.

Silverman, Janis. *Help Me Say Goodbye: Activities for Helping Kids Cope When a Special Person Dies*. Minnesota: Fairview Press, 1999.

Macgregor, Cynthia. *Why Do People Die? Helping Your Child Understand with Love and Illustrations*. New Jersey: Carol Publishing Group, 1999.

BOOKS FOR CHILDREN AGES 9–12

Greenlee, Sharon. *When Someone Dies*. Georgia: Peachtree Press, 1992.

Dougy Center Staff. *35 Ways to Help a Grieving Child*. Oregon: The Dougy Center for Grieving Children, 1999.

BOOKS FOR TEENAGERS

Wolfelt, Alan D., Ph.D. *Healing Your Grieving Heart for Teens*. Colorado: Companion Press, 2001.

Gootman, Marilyn. *When a Friend Dies: A Book for Teens About Grieving & Healing*. Minnesota: Free Spirit Publishing, 1994.

BOOKS FOR PARENTS

Johnson, Joy, and Marvin Johnson. *Children Grieve, Too: A Book for Families Who Have Experienced a Death*. Nebraska: Centering Corp., 1998.

Grollman, Earl A. *Talking About Death: A Dialogue Between Parent and Child.* Boston: Beacon Press, 1991.

Grollman, Early A. *Explaining Death to Children.* Boston: Beacon Press, 1967.

Kubler-Ross, Elisabeth. *On Children and Death.* New York: Collier Press, 1983.

Schafer, Dan, and Christine Lyons. *How Do We Tell the Children? A Step-by-Step Guide for Helping Children Two to Teen Cope When Someone Dies.* New York: Newmarket Press, 1993.

Hanniford, Mary Jo, and Michael H. Popkin. *Windows: Healing and Helping Through Loss.* Atlanta: Active Parenting Publishers, 1992.

ORGANIZATIONS AND WEB SITES

www.death-dying.com

Association for Death Education
and Counseling
342 North Main Street
West Hartford, CT 06117-2507
860/586-7503
Fax: 860/586-7550
www.adec.org

U.S. Department of Transportation,
Inc.
National Highway Traffic Safety
Administration
400 Seventh Street SW
Washington, DC 20590
www.dot.gov/

www.anxietytofreedom.com

Anxiety Disorders Association of
America
11900 Parklawn Drive, Suite 100
Rockville, MD 20852
www.adaa.org

Social Phobia/Social Anxiety
Associaton
5025 N. Central Avenue #421
Phoenix, AZ 85012
www.social/phobia.org

www.anxieties.com

Chapter 7: Divorce

BOOKS FOR CHILDREN AGES 4-8

Lansky, Vicky. *It's Not Your Fault, Koko Bear: A Read-Together Book for Parents & Young Children During Divorce*. Minnesota: Book Peddlers, 1998.

Nightingale, Lois V. *My Parents Still Love Me Even Though They're Getting Divorced: An Interactive Tale for Children*. California: Nightingale Rose, 1997.

Haughton, Emma. *Rainy Day*. Minnesota: Carolrhoda Books, 2000.

Stinsoin, Kathy. *Mom & Dad Don't Live Together Anymore*. Toronto: Annick Press, Ltd., 1997.

Girard, Linda Walyvoord. *At Daddy's on Saturdays*. Illinois: Albert Whitman & Co., 1987.

Krementz, Jill. *How It Feels When Parents Divorce*. New York: Knopf, 1984.

BOOKS FOR CHILDREN AGES 9–12

Thomas, Shirley, and Dorothy Rankin. *Divorced but Still My Parents*. New York: Springboard Publications, 1998.

Prolop, Michael S. *Divorce Happens to the Nicest Kids: A Self-Help Book for Kids*. Ohio: Alegra House Publishers, 1996.

Stern, Zoe, and Evan Stern. *Divorce Is Not the End of the World: Zoe's and Evan's Coping Guide for Kids*. California: Tricycle Press, 1997.

Margolis, Bette S. *A Heart Full of Love*. Colorado: Bette's Books, 1999.

BOOKS FOR TEENAGERS

Hunt, Angela Elwell. *Keeping Your Life Together When Your Parents Pull Apart: A Teen's Guide to Surviving Divorce*. California: Universe.com, Inc., 2000.

Bokowski, Sara. *Teens are Non-Divorceable: A Workbook for Divorced Parents and Their Chidren: Ages 12–18*. Illinois: ACTA Publications, 1990.

BOOKS FOR PARENTS

Lansky, Vicki. *Vicki Lansky's Divorce Book for Parents: Helping Your Children Cope with Divorce and Its Aftermath*. Minnesota: Book Peddlers, 1996.

Boyan, Susan, and Ann Marie Termini. *Cooperative Parenting and Divorce*. Atlanta: Active Parenting Publishers.

Kimball, Gayle. *How to Survive Your Parents' Divorce: Kids' Advice to Kids*. California: Equality Press, 1994.

Benedek, Elissa P., M.D., and Catherine F. Brown, M.D. *How to Help Your Child Overcome Your Divorce: A Support Guide for Families*. New York: Newmarket Press, 2001.

Schneider, Meg F., and Joan Zuckerberg, Ph.D. *Difficult Questions Kids Ask—and Are Too Afraid to Ask—About Divorce*. New York: Simon & Schuster, 1996.

Chapter 8: Driving
BOOKS FOR TEENS AND PARENTS

Berardelli, Phil. *Safe Young Drivers 2000: A Guide for Parents and Teens*. Virginia: Nautilus Communications, Inc., 2000.

ORGANIZATIONS AND WEB SITES

AAA Foundation for Traffic Safety
1440 New York Ave NW
Suite 201
Washington, DC 20005
Tel: 202/638-5944
Fax: 202/638-5943
Order Fulfillment Center:
1-800-305-SAFE
www.aaafts.org

Teen New Drivers
www.teendriving.com

National Sleep Foundation
www.sleepfoundation.org

Mothers Against Drunk Driving
www.madd.org

The National Highway Traffic Safety Administration (NHTSA)
www.nhtsa.dot.gov

Chapter 9: Friends
BOOKS FOR CHILDREN AGES 4–8

Lobel, Arnold. *Frog and Toad Are Friends*. New York: HarperCollins Children's Books, 1979.

Leonard, Marcia, and Dorothy Handelman (Illustrator). *Best Friends*. Connecticut: Millbrook Press Trade, 1999.

BOOKS FOR CHILDREN AGES 9–12

Lonnie, Michelle and Teresa McHugh (Illustrator). *How Kids Make Friends: Secrets for Making Lots of Friends, No Matter How Shy You Are*. Illinios: Freedom Publisher Co., 1997.

BOOKS FOR TEENAGERS

Scott, Sharon. *How to Say No and Keep Your Friends: Peer Pressure Reversal for Teens and Preteens*. Massachusetts: Human Resource Development Press, 1997.

BOOKS FOR PARENTS

Nowicki, Stephen, Jr., and Marshall Duke. *Helping the Child Who Doesn't Fit In*. Atlanta, GA: Peachtree Publishers, Ltd., 1992.

Osman, Betty B., in association with Henriette Blinder. *No One to Play With: The Social Side of Learning Disabilities*. New York: Random House, 1982.

Chapter 10: Illness and Disability

BOOKS FOR CHILDREN 4–8

Fassler, Joan, and Joe Lasker (Illustrator). *Howie Helps Himself*. Illinios: Albert Whitman & Co., 1987.

Thompson, Mary. *Andy and His Yellow Frisbee*. Maryland: Woodbine House, 1996.

Fleming, Virginia. *Be Good to Eddie Lee*. New York: Philomel Books, 1993.

Galvin, Matthew. *Otto Learns About His Medicine: A Story About Medication for Hyperactive Children*. New York: Magination Press/ Brunner Mazel, 1995.

Fassler, David, and Kelly McQueen. *What's a Virus Anyway? The Kids' Book About AIDS*. Burlington, VT: Waterfront Books, 1990.

BOOKS FOR CHILDREN AGES 9–12

Cutler, Jane. *Spaceman*. New York: Viking Penguin, 1999.

Kachur, Wanda Gilberts. *The Nautilus*. Minnesota: Peytral Publications, 1997.

Benton, Hope. *Whoa, Nellie!* Ohio: Open Minds, Inc., 1996.

Schneider, Meg F. *Help! My Teacher Hates Me: How to Survive Poor Grades, a Friend Who Cheats Off You, Oral Reports and More*. New York: Workman Publishing, 1995.

Gordon, Michael. *My Brother's a World-Class Pain: A Sibling's Guide to ADHD/Hyperactivity.* New York: GSI Publications, Inc., 1992.

BOOKS FOR TEENAGERS

Bruch, Hilde. *The Golden Cage: The Enigma of Anorexia Nervosa.* Cambridge, Massachusetts: Harvard University Press, 1978.

Lieberman, Susan Abel. *The Real High School Handbook: How to Survive, Thrive, and Prepare for What's Next.* Massachusetts: Houghton Mifflin, 1997.

Quinn, Patricia O., M.D. *ADD and the College Student: A Guide for High School and College Students.* New York: Magination, 1994.

BOOKS FOR PARENTS

Smith, Corinne, Ph.D., and Lisa Strict. *Learning Disabilities A to Z: A Parent's Complete Guide to Learning Disabilities from Preschool to Adulthood.* New York: Simon & Schuster, 1999.

Faber, Adele, and Elaine Mazlish. *How to Talk So Kids Can Learn: At Home and In School.* New York: Fireside, 1996.

Sacker, Ira M., and Marc A. Zimmer. *Dying to Be Thin: Understanding & Defeating Anorexia & Bulimia.* New York: Warner Books, 1995.

Siegel, Michelle, and Judith Brisman. *Surviving an Eating Disorder: Strategies for Family and Friends.* New York: HarperCollins, 1997.

Barkley, Russell A. *Attention Deficit Hyperactivity Disorder: A Handbook for Diagnosis and Treatment.* New York: The Guilford Press, 1990.

DuPaul, George J., and Gary Stoner. *ADHD in the Schools: Assessment and Intervention Strategies.* New York: The Guilford Press, 1994.

Fowler, Mary Cahill. *Maybe You Know My Kid: A Parents' Guide to Identifying, Understanding and Helping Your Child with Attention Deficit Hyperactivity Disorder.* New York: Birch Lane Press, published by Carol Publishing Group, 1990.

Garber, Stephen W., Marianne Daniels Garber, and Robyn F. Spizman. *If Your Child is Hyperactive, Inattentive, Impulsive, Distractible: Helping the ADD Child.* New York: Villard, Random House, 1990.

Garber, Stephen W., Marianne Daniels Garber, and Robyn F. Spizman *Beyond Ritalin: Facts About Medication and Other Strategies for Helping Children, Adolescents, and Adults with Attention Deficit Disorders.* New York: Villard, Random House, 1996.

Hallowell, Edward M., M.D., and John J. Ratey, M.D. *Driven to Distraction*. New York: Pantheon Books, 1994.

Hallowell, Edward M., M.D., and John J. Ratey, M.D. *Answers to Distraction*. New York: Pantheon Books, 1994.

Hartmann, Thom, Foreword by Michael Popkin. *Attention Deficit Disorder: A Different Perception*. Penn Valley, CA: Underwood-Millerm 1993.

Hartmann, Thom, *Thom Hartmann's Complete Guide to ADHD*. Grass Valley, CA: Underwood Books, 2000.

Parker, Harvey C. *The ADD Hyperactivity Workbook for Parents, Teachers, and Kids*. Plantation, FL: Specialty Press, 1994.

ORGANIZATIONS AND WEB SITES

Compassionate Friends
P.O. Box 3696
Oak Brook, IL 60522-3696
www.compassionatefriends.com

**National Education Association-
Health Information Network**
1201 16th Street, NW, Suite 521
Washington, DC 20036
202/822-7570, 1-800-718-8387
Fax: 202/822-7775
www.nea.org/hin

**National Eating Disorders
Association**
1-800-931-2237
*www.kidsource.com/nedo/index.
html*

**CDC National Prevention
Information Network**
800/458-5231
www.cdcnpin.org

Mothers' Voices
165 W. 46th Street, Suite 701
New York, NY 10036
212/730-2777
www.mvoices.org

American Medical Association
515 N. State Street
Chicago, IL 60610
312/464-5000
www.ama-assn.org

Advocates for Youth
1025 Vermont Avenue, NW,
Suite 200
Washington, DC 20005
202/347-5700
www.advocatesforyouth.org

American Academy of Pediatrics
141 Northwest Point Boulevard
Elk Grove Village, IL 60007-1098
847/434-4000
Fax: 847/434-8000
www.aap.org

**American Anorexia/Bulimia
Association, Inc.**
165 West 46th Street, Suite 1108
New York, NY 10036
212/575-6200
www.aabainc.org

AIDS Action
1906 Sunderland Place NW
Washington, DC 20036
202/530-8030
Fax: 202/530-8031
www.aidsaction.org

AIDS Action Committee
131 Clarendon Street
Boston, MA 02116
617/437-6200
Fax: 617/437-6445
Hotline: 1-800-235-2331
Youth Hotline: 1-800-788-1234
www.aac.org

American Red Cross
www.redcross.org

**National Prevention Information
Network**
P.O. Box 6003
Rockville, MD 20849-6003
1-800-458-5231
Fax: 1-888-282-7681
www.cdcnpin.org

**National Information Center for
Children and Youth with
Disabilities**
P.O. Box 1492

Washington, DC 20013
1-800-695-0285
Fax: 202/884-8441
http://nichcy.org

**American Psychological
Association**
750 First Street, NE
Washington, DC 20002-4242
1-800-374-2721
www.apa.org

**Association for Children and
Adults with Learning Disabilities**
412/881-2253

**The National Information Center
for the Handicapped**
P.O. Box 1492
Washington, DC 20013

**Children and Adults with Attention
Deficit Disorder**
C.H.A.D.D.
1-800-233-4050 voicemail only
www.chadd.org

International Dyslexia Association
1-800-ABCD-123 leave message only

**National Center for Learning
Disabilities**
NCLD
381 Park Avenue South, Suite 1401
New York, NY 10016
888/575-7373
Fax: 212/545-9665
www.ncld.org

Learning Disabilities Association of America
LDA
4156 Library Road
Pittsburgh, PA 15234-1349
412/341-1515 (voice mail)
Fax: 412/344-0224
www.ldanatl.org

Attention Deficit Disorder Association
ADDA
847/432-ADDA
www.add.org

Chapter 11: Money and Work

BOOKS FOR CHILDREN AGES 4–8

Berenstain, Stan and Jan Berenstain. *The Berenstain Bears' Trouble with Money.* New York: Random House, Inc., 1983.

BOOKS FOR CHILDREN AGES 9–12

Godfrey, Neale S., and Randy Verougstraete. *Neale S. Godfrey's Ultimate Kids' Money Book.* New York: Simon & Schuster, 1998.

Honig, Debbie, and Stephen Lewis (Illustrator). *Growing Money: A Complete Investing Guide for Kids.* New York: Penguin Putnam Books, 1999.

BOOKS FOR TEENAGERS

Kiyosaki, Robert T., and Sharon L. Lechter. *Rich Dad, Poor Dad: What the Rich Teach Their Kids About Money—That the Poor and Middle Class Do Not!* New York: Warner Books, Inc., 2000.

Burkett, Larry, Marnie Wooding, and Chris Kielesinski. *Money Matters for Teens.* Illnois: Moody Press, 2001.

Covey, Sean. *The 7 Habits of Highly Effective Teens: The Ultimate Teenage Success Guide.* New York: Simon & Schuster, 1998.

ORGANIZATIONS AND WEB SITES

National Prevention Information Network
P.O. Box 6003

Rockville, MD 20849-6003
1-800-458-5231
www.cdcnpin.org

Chapter 12: Sexuality

BOOKS FOR CHILDREN AGES 4–8

Cole, Joanne. *How You Were Born*. New Jersey: Wilmor, Inc., 1993.

Meredith, Susan. *Where Do Babies Come From?* Oklahoma: Usborne Starting Point Science, 1991.

Nilson, Lennart. *How Was I Born?* New York: Dell Trade, 1993.

Brown, Laurie Krasny, and Marc Brown. *What's the Big Secret? Talking About Sex With Girls and Boys*. New York: Little, Brown, 1997.

Gordon, Sol and Judith Gordon. *Did the Sun Shine Before You Were Born?* New York: Prometheus Books, 1990.

Andry, Andrew, and Steven Schepp. *How Babies Are Made*. Boston: Little, Brown, 1968.

BOOKS FOR CHILDREN AGES 9–12

Westheimer, Ruth K., and Diane Degroat (Illustrator). *Dr. Ruth Talks to Kids: Where You Came From, How Your Body Changes, and What Sex Is All About*. California: Aladdin Paperbacks, 1998.

Gravelle, Karen, Jennifer Gravelle, and Debbie Palen (Illustrator). *The Period Book: Everything You Don't Want to Ask (But Need to Know)*. New York: Walker & Co., 1996.

Gravelle, Karen, Nick Castro (Contributor), and Robert Leighton, (Illustrator). *What's Going on Down There: Answers to Questions Boys Find Hard to Ask*. New York: Walker & Co., 1998.

Harris, Robie. *It's Perfectly Normal: Changing Bodies, Sex, and Sexual Health*. Massachusetts: Candlewick Press, 1994.

Madaras, Lynda. *What's Happening to My Body? Book for Girls: A Growing Up Guide for Parents and Daughters*. New York: Newmarket Press, 2000.

Madaras, Lynda. *What's Happening to My Body? Book for Boys: A Growing Up Guide for Parents and Sons*. New York: Newmarket Press, 2000.

BOOKS FOR TEENAGERS

Bell, Ruth. *Changing Bodies, Changing Lives: A Book for Teens on Sex and Relationships*. New York: Times Books, 1998.

Rench, Janice E. *Understanding Sexual Identity: A Book for Gay and Lesbian Teens and Their Friends*. Minnesota: Lerner Publishing Group, 1992.

BOOKS FOR PARENTS

Basso, Michael J. *The Underground Guide to Teenage Sexuality: An Essential Handbook for Today's Teens & Parents*. Minnesota: Fairview Press, 1997.

ORGANIZATIONS AND WEB SITES

Planned Parenthood Federation of America
810 Seventh Avenue
New York, NY 10019
212/541-7800
www.plannedparenthood.org

Parents, Families, and Friends of Lesbians and Gays
1726 M Street NW, Suite 400
Washington, DC 20036
www.pflag.org

ETR Associates
P.O. Box 1830
Santa Cruz, CA 95061-1830
831/438-4060
www.etr.org

American Library Association
50 East Huron Street
Chicago, IL 60611
1-800-545-2433
www.ala.org

Chapter 13: Tobacco

BOOKS FOR CHILDREN AGES 4–8

Brenneman, Tim C. *Jimmie Boogie Learns About Smoking*. Ohio: Grand Unification Press, 2000.

BOOKS FOR TEENAGERS

Lang, Susan S., and Beth H. Marks. *Teens and Tobacco: A Fatal Attraction*. Colorado: Twenty First Century Books, 1996.

BOOKS FOR PARENTS

Schwebel, Robert, and Benjamin Spock. *Saying No Is Not Enough: What to Say and How to Listen to Your Kids about Alcohol, Tobacco, and Other Drugs—A Step-by-Step Guide for Parents of Children Aged Three through Ten*. New York: Newmarket Press, 1998.

Schwebel, Robert Ph.D. *How to Help Your Kids Choose to be Tobacco Free: A Guide for Parents of Children Ages 3 through 19*. New York: Newmarket Press, 1999.

ORGANIZATIONS AND WEB SITES

Campaign for Tobacco-Free Kids
1400 Eye Street NW, Suite 1200
Washington, DC 20005
202/296-5469
www.tobaccofreekids.org

**Take 10: Start Talking So Your
Kids Don't Smoke**
www.2take.10.com

**Center for Disease Control and
Prevention**
Tobacco Information and
Prevention Source (TIPS)
www.cdc.gov/tobacco

Chapter 14: Violence and Safety

BOOKS FOR CHILDREN AGES 4–8

Girard, Linda Walvoord. *Who Is a Stranger and What Should I Do?* Illinois: Albert Whitman, 1993.

Agassi, Martine, and Marieka Heinlen (Illustrator). *Hands Are Not for Hitting.* Minnesota: Free Spirit Publishing, Inc., 1999.

Berenstain, Stan, and Jan Berenstain. *The Berenstain Bears and No Guns Allowed.* New York: Random House Books for Young Readers, 2000.

BOOKS FOR TEENAGERS

Kay, Phillip, Andrea Estepa, and Al Desetta. *Things Get Hectic: Teens Write About the Violence that Surrounds Them.* New York: Simon & Schuster Trade, 1998.

Levy, Barrie. *In Love and in Danger: A Teen's Guide to Breaking Free of Abusive Relationships.* Washington: Seal Press, 1998.

Murray, John Michael. *Think About It: Understanding The Impact of TV/Movie Violence.* Georgia: Active Parenting Publishers, 2001.

BOOKS FOR PARENTS

Capello, Dominic. *Ten Talks Parents Must Have with Their Children About Violence.* New York: Hyperion, 2000.

ORGANIZATIONS AND WEB SITES

Center to Prevent Handgun Violence
1225 Eye Street, NW, Suite 1100
Washington, DC 20005
202/898-0792
Fax: 202/371-9615
www.handguncontrol.org

Educators for Social Responsibility
23 Garden Street
Cambridge, MA 02138
617/492-1764
www.esrnational.org

Institute for Mental Health Initiatives
Channeling Children's Anger
2175 K Street, NW, Suite 700
Washington, DC 20037
202/467-2285
www.imhi.org

National Injury and Violence Prevention Resource Center
Children Safety Network
Education Development Center, Inc.
55 Chapel Street
Newton, MA 02458-1060
617/969-7100
www.edc.org

Join Together: A National Resource for Communities Fighting Substance Abuse and Gun Violence
441 Stuart Street, 7th Fl.

Boston, MA 02116
617/437-1500
Fax: 617/437-9394
E-mail: *info@jointogether.org*
www.jointogether.org

Prevent Child Abuse America
www.preventchildabuse.org

National Center on Child Abuse and Neglect
P.O. Box 1182
Washington, DC 20013
301/251-5157

Child Find, Inc.
7 Innis Avenue
New Paltz, NY 12561
www.childfind.org

Parents Anonymous
www.parentsanonymous.org

National Clearinghouse on Child Abuse and Neglect Information
P.O. Box 1182
Washington, DC 20013-1182
703/385-7565
1-800-394-3366
Fax: 703/385-3206
nccanch@calib.com

ADDITIONAL PARENTING BOOKS AND VIDEOTAPES

Borba, Michele. *Parents Do Make a Difference: How to Raise Kids with Solid Character, Strong Minds & Caring Hearts*. California: Jossey-Bass, 1999.

Conners, C. Keith. *Feeding the Brain: How Foods Affect Children*. New York and London: Plenum Press, 1989.

Elium, Jeanne, and Don Elium. *Raising a Teenager: Parents and the Nurturing of a Responsible Teen*. California: Celestial Arts, 1999.

Faber, Adele, and Elaine Mazlish. *How to Talk So Kids Will Listen & How to Listen So Kids Will Talk*. Mamaroneck, NY: International Center for Creative Thinking, 1990.

Garber, Stephen, Ph.D., Marianne Garber, Ph.D., and Robyn Freedman Spizman. *Good Behavior*. New York: St. Martin's Press, 1992.

Miller, Jamie. *10-Minute Life Lessons for Kids: 52 Fun and Simple Game and Activities to Teach Your Children Honesty, Trust, Love and Other Important Values*. New York: Harper Perennial Library, 1998.

Nolte, Dorothy Law. *Children Learn What They Live: Parenting to Inspire Values*. New York: Workman Publishing, 1998.

Popkin, Michael H. *1,2,3,4 Parents!* (in Spanish as: *1,2,3,4 Padres!*) book and video, Atlanta: Active Parenting Publishers, 1996.

Popkin, Michael H. *Active Parenting of Teens*. Parent's guide. Atlanta: Active Parenting Publishers, 1990.

Popkin, Michael H. *Active Parenting of Teens*. Video-based Program. Atlanta: Active Parenting Publishers, 1998.

Popkin, Michael H. *Active Parenting Today*. Parent's guide. Atlanta: Active Parenting Publishers, 1993.

Popkin, Michael H. *Active Parenting Today* (in Spanish as: *Padres Activos de Hoy)* Video-based Program. Atlanta: Active Parenting Publishers, 1993.

Popkin, Michael H., and Susan Greathead. *Free the Horses: A Self-Esteem Adventure*. Atlanta: Active Parenting Publishers, 1991.

Popkin, Michael H., Bettie Youngs, and Jane Healy. *Helping Your Child Succeed in School*. Atlanta: Active Parenting Publishers, 1995.

Popkin, Michael H., Bettie Youngs, and Jane Healy. *Parents on Board: Building Academic Success Through Parent Involvement*. Video. Atlanta: Active Parenting Publishers, 1995.

Popkin, Michael H., and Kathryn Vander. *She Said Yes: The Unlikely Martyrdom of Cassie Bernall*. Video. Atlanta: Active Parenting Publishers, 1999.

Popkin, Michael, H, and Peggy Hendrickson. *Parent's Guide: Families In Action*. Atlanta: Active Parenting Publishers, 2000.

Schaefer, Charles Ph.D., and Theresa DiGeronomo, M.Ed. *How to Talk to Your Kids About Really Important Things For Children 4 to 12*. Calfornia: Jossey-Bass, 1994.

Trujillo, Michelle L. *Why Can't We Talk? What Teens Would Share if Parents Would Listen*. Florida: Health Communications, 2000.

PARENTING ORGANIZATIONS AND WEB SITES

Active Parenting
810-B Franklin Court
Marietta, GA 30067
1-800-825-0060
www.activeparenting.com

SIECUS
130 W. 42nd Street, Suite 350
New York, NY 10036-7802
212/819-9770
www.siecus.org/parent/index.html

National Council for Adoption
Children's Research and
Information Center
1930 17th Street, NW
Washington, DC 20009-6207
202/328-1200
www.ncfa-usa.org

National Adoption Information Clearinghouse
888/251-0075
www.calib.com/naic

Girls, Incorporated
120 Wall Street
New York, NY 10005-3902
1-800-374-4475
www.girlsinc.org

Child Welfare League of America
440 First Street, NW, 3rd Floor
Washington, DC 20001-2085
202/638-2952
Fax: 202/638-4004
www.cwla.org

The National Parenting Center
www.tnpc.com

StepFamily Association of America, Inc.
650 J Street
Suite 205
Lincoln, NE 68508
1-800-735-0329
Fax: 402/477-8317
www.stepfam.org

National Association for the
Education of Young Children
1509 16th Street NW
Washington, DC 20036-1426

1-800-424-2460
Fax: 202/328-1846
www.naeyc.org

The Active Parenting Resource Catalog
Containing more than 300 books and video resources for parents and
professionals, including many listed in this resource section, the catalog is
available free of charge. Contact:

Active Parenting Publishers
810-B Franklin Court
Marietta, GA 30067
Phone: 1-800-825-0060
Fax: 770-429-0334

E-mail: *cservice@activeparenting.com*
or view the entire catalog online at
www.activeparenting.com

Endnotes

Chapter 4.

1. *Half of the college students who were victims:* Towson State University Center for Study and Prevention of Campus Violence, MD, 1990. Neadd.org Web page.
2. *Greater risk for HIV infection or pregnancy:* Hingson, R. W. L. Strunin, et al., "Beliefs about AIDS, Use of Alcohol and Drugs, and Unprotected Sex Among Massachusetts Adolescents." *Amer. J. of Public Health,* 3/90, p. 295–299. Neadd.org Web site.
3. *Less than 1 percent of those who have tried it:* Gladwell, Malcomb. (2001) *The Tipping Point: How Little Things Can Make a Big Difference,* Little, Brown & Company.
4. *54 percent who have used any illegal substances:* University of Michigan's Monitoring the Future study, 2000.

Chapter 5.

1. *According to researchers Schacter and McCauley. When your child is afraid,* Simon and Schuster. From North Dakota State University Web site.
2. Garber, Stephen W., Ph.D., Marianne Daniels Garber and Robyn Freedman Spizman. *Monsters Under the Bed and Other Childhood Fears: Helping Your Child Overcome Anxieties, Fears, and Phobias.* New York: Villard Books, 1993.

Chapter 6.

2. *One in twenty children under the age of eighteen:* US Bureau of Census, 1990.
3. *19 percent of these children showed serious problems:* Worden, J. William and

Phyllis S. Silverman, 1996. "Parental Death and Adjustment of School-Age Children." Omega 33:2, 91–102.

Chapter 8.
1. *About 5,000 teenagers a year:* Wisely, Dale. The American Academy of Pediatrics. www.chiffandfipple.com/driving/facts.htm.
2. *People 16 to 20:* Wisely, Dale. The American Academy of Pediatrics. www.chiffandfipple.com/driving/facts.htm.
3. *Sixteen-year-olds are twenty times more likely:* Wisely, Dale. The American Academy of Pediatrics. www.chiffandfipple.com/driving/facts.htm.
4. *At least half of teen accidents:* Insurance Institute for Highway Safety and the National Highway Safety Administration (U.S.D.O.T.) http://howismyteen driving.net/page2.html.
5. *Teen boys are twice as likely:* Insurance Institute for Highway Safety and the National Highway Safety Administration (U.S.D.O.T.) http://howismyteen driving.net/page2.html

Chapter 9.
3. *Researchers such as:* Baumrind, D. "Current Patterns of Parental Authority." *Developmental Psychology Monographs* 4 (1971): 1–103.

Chapter 10.
1. *With approximately 5.5 million children:* National Center for Learning Disabilities. www.ncld.org/info/index.cfm.
2. *Possess an increased sense of maturity and responsibility:* Powel and Ogle, 1985.www.ldonline.org.
3. *Estimates of eating disorders running as high as 10%:* American Academy of Child & Adolescent Psychiatry; 8/98, www.aacap.org/publications/factsfam/ eating.htm.
4. *25 percent of his calories through French fries: www.parents-talk.com/ meetingsofthemind/expertsadvice/article=_archive/healthy=_eating.* 10/19/00.

Chapter 12.
2. *Only about 2 percent of them were really gay:* Remafedi, G. et al. (1992) "Demography of sexual orientation in adolescents." *Pediatrics,* vol. 89, April 1992, 714–721.

Chapter 13.
1. *A study at the University of Michigan:* Gladwell, Malcomb. (2001) *The Tipping Point: How Little Things Can Make a Big Difference*, Little, Brown & Company, page 234.

2. *Sensation seekers also fit the profile of the typical heavy smoker:* Gladwell, Malcomb. (2001) *The Tipping Point: How Little Things Can Make a Big Difference,* Little, Brown & Company, page 232.
3. *Temporarily treating the depression:* Gladwell, Malcomb. (2001) *The Tipping Point: How Little Things Can Make a Big Difference,* Little, Brown & Company, page 246.
4. *Higher incidence of smoking in psychiatric patients:* Gladwell, Malcomb. (2001) *The Tipping Point: How Little Things Can Make a Big Difference,* Little, Brown & Company, page 245.
5. *90 percent of smokers began before the age of 18:* "Preventing tobacco use among young people: A Report of the Surgeon General, U.S. Dept. of Health and Human Services, 1994. www.tobaccofreekids.org.
6. *Teens who said their parents would be upset:* AP Jan 2001, a study by Bruce Simons-Morton, National Institutes of Health.
7. *78 percent of teenage boys said: Parenting Today's Teen-Family Journal: Teens and smoking. www.parentingteens.com/familyjournal.shtml.* Page 3.

Chapter 14.

1. John Michael Murray in his documentary video *Think About It: The Impact of Media Violence.* Active Parenting Publishers, 2001.

Index